Singing
and
The Actor

Gillyanne Kayes

A & C Black • London
Theatre Arts Books / Routledge • New York

First published in 2000 by
A & C Black (Publishers) Limited
35 Bedford Row, London WC1R 4JH

© 2000 Gillyanne Kayes

ISBN 0-7136-4888-0

A CIP catalogue record for this book is available from the
British Library.

Published in the USA in 2000 by
Theatre Arts Books / Routledge
29 West 35th Street, New York, NY 10001

USA ISBN 0-878-30106-2

CIP available from the Library of Congress.

Cover photograph: Cabaret by Colin Willoughby/Arena Images
Designed by Susan McIntyre
Line drawings by Joanna Cameron © Joanna Cameron
Diagrams 4 and 13-23, Chapter 8, and Placement diagram, Chapter
11 by Rick Lipton © Rick Lipton
Diagrams 5-12, Chapter 8, reproduced by permission from *Elements of
Acoustic Phonetics* by Peter Ladefoged published by The University of
Chicago Press.
Edited by Ana Sanderson

Typeset in 10 on 12pt Photina.
Printed and bound in Great Britain by Creative Print and Design
(Wales), Ebbw Vale

Contents

Acknowledgements

Jo Estill is not the only person whose work I would like to acknowledge in this book. Chapters 8 and 11 have had considerable input from my colleague Rick Lipton, a young and talented voice nerd (his description, not mine!) who manages to infect those around him with his passion for phonetics. Rick and I spent many hours discussing the principles of medialisation, and he has prepared all the diagrams dealing with this topic. I'd also like to thank Meribeth Bunch for her encouragement given to me particularly in the early stages of writing, as well as for discussions about breath use. Jacob Lieberman, an osteopath specialising in manipulating the laryngeal muscles, gave me many insights on the tongue and jaw, and it is from workshops with him that I learned about laryngeal orienteering. Other colleagues have contributed by reading chapters for me and spending time talking me through their observations: Tom and Sara Harris, John Rubin, Chris Kell, Paul Farrington, Janice Chapman and Jeremy Fisher (who read everything as I wrote the first draft). I have been fortunate enough to have a guardian angel for an editor. Without Ana the book would never have come into being anyway, since she was the one who put me up for it. Thank you for believing in me and for your understanding of my work. Last but by no means least, I thank all my students – past and present – to whom this book is dedicated, because teaching is two-way traffic.

The phonetics and system of transcription for Standard British and American used in this book are drawn from a number of sources, including the new *Handbook of the International Phonetic Association* (1999), Wells (1990), Roach (1991), Kenyon and Knott (1953), Barton and Dal Vera (1995), Fairbanks (1960), and Skinner (1990), among others. Certain conventions of transcription have been adopted, such as the distinction between the initial vowel component in the diphthong [eɪ] and the short vowel [ɛ]. The objective has been to devise a phonetic system that provides the speaker with as many usable contrastive vowel sounds as possible. The principle of interpretative spelling derives from Herman and Herman (1943) and is used to communicate phonetic ideas without the use of unfamiliar symbols.

The author and publishers would like to thank the following who gave permission for the inclusion of copyright material.

Introduction

When I mentioned to a student of mine who had been away on tour that I was completing a book on singing, he said, 'Oh, great! A book on singing for actors! That's just what we need. Most of us are blaguing our way through the singing out there, and we really need this kind of information.' He is a successful performer, charismatic on stage, and he has a good voice. Like many others, he had been getting by on instinct when he came to see me, and wanted to know more. This book is about the 'more'.

Singing is not really a gift. Anyone can do it if they work hard enough. Nor is it 'natural', though we all have the equipment to do it. The desire to sing – to express ourselves through sustained sound and the medium of song – is instinctive and natural. The larynx, however, is set up to fulfil another primary function, so in this sense we cannot say that the act of singing is natural. Is singing less natural than speaking? Not in terms of that primary functioning of the larynx, though, again, the need to communicate feels very natural and is so important to us that as children we learn complex manoeuvres of speech at a very early stage in our development.

There is a way in which singing is more difficult than ordinary speech: it requires us to sustain pitch, to hold our breath, and to manoeuvre the pipe of our vocal tract like a musical instrument. This is what we hear when we remark that 'so-and-so has a good voice'. And it can be learned. Essentially this is the purpose of this book: to dispel the myths about singing, to offer a template for training, and, in particular, to focus on a training that is practical and appropriate for a singing actor.

My journey

In common with many singing teachers, I started off life as a professional singer and musician. What I learned very quickly, as I began to teach, was that being able to do it yourself is no guarantee of being a good teacher. I worked with all kinds of people – people who wanted to sing at the local pub (this was pre-karaoke), terrified ex-bathroom singers (many of them aged sixty and over, and willing to have a go at anything I asked them to do), choral singers, and, of course, training actors. It was particularly with the last group that I began to develop a way of working. For one thing, I was forced to find a way of working with people in groups, which was very different from my own training as a classical singer. Group work is far more challenging than one-to-one, for which you can use the guru approach. Actors are also very aware and perceptive; if you present them with a muddled, unclear approach, eventually they will spot it, no matter how scary the process of singing might be for them. I also saw, with actors, a generosity towards each other in their learning and a shared excitement about the act of performing that, sadly, is often lacking in more conventional singing training. During this period in my life I was lucky enough to work alongside some very fine voice trainers, and I owe them a lot in my attempts to structure the work that I was then teaching. I had one guiding principle throughout my years in drama training – that everyone has the ability to sing. Probably more than anything, this fired me to work out what happens when we sing well, and it made me curious about the vocal mechanism.

In 1992, the renowned teacher and voice researcher, Jo Estill, came into my life. I think it is fair to say that Jo's work made a big impact on the theatre scene in the UK because it offered an alternative approach to the traditional way of singing training. Already, with ten years of teaching behind me, I found that Jo was able to explain and analyse the way we use our voices with an authority and clarity that no book, no teacher, and no one person who theorised about voice had done before. Here was a teacher who had done it, could still do it, and who could explain what she was doing step-by-step! I think that we will only understand the full effect Jo's training model – *Voice Craft with Compulsory Figures* – when we are well into the next millennium.

Training in the Estill model undoubtedly made me a better teacher. I now had to rely less on patience and positive noises in my teaching – I knew what I was hearing and what to do about it. I have consistently found that actors love this work because it is quick, it is not dependent on musicianship (it works on the mechanics of the voice first), and because there is no aesthetic bias. Anyone can do it, and all types of music and sounds are OK so long as they are non-abusive. Readers who are familiar with the Estill model will recognise a substantial body of Jo's work in this book; it appears with her knowledge and approval. I could not have written the book without including this material because it is what I teach.

As a result of working so closely with Jo Estill, my career pattern has changed. Although I still do classes for actors, pop and classical singers (individual and group work), I now run a company which is committed to the spread of knowledge about the voice. We run training seminars for teachers, performers and voice therapists all the year round throughout the UK, and we are branching out into Europe. Teaching is an enormous challenge and a responsibility; it is very important to me that I reach the teachers as they are the ones who will teach you!

Why this book?

To a large extent vocal pedagogy is based on the classical singing tradition. This is true of knowledge received via the tradition of performance practice, and of most research studies. Stanislavsky recommended that actors study the craft of opera singers, presumably in order to master the art of projection: opera singers must project above an orchestra without amplification, and this may be one reason why singers in the theatre have continued to seek out classical singing teachers in order to learn how to sing 'properly'. 'Properly' is the key word here, and, I believe, should be substituted by 'appropriately'. Until recently, actors and musical theatre singers have been offered training that is essentially a watered-down version of a classical singing training. This is neither appropriate nor adequate to the needs of modern theatre.

Classical singers are trained to sing beautifully. Their instrument must be so well honed that, even when they are portraying angry or sad, the sound is still in the larger context of beautiful singing. In very broad terms, this is what we mean by 'bel canto'. Within this context there are certain requirements of good classical singing that have developed to meet the demands of the music that is sung by classical singers and the houses they perform in. Actors are working in a very different environment. Our musical theatre writers are not writing classical music, so it doesn't make sense to sing this music classically. Musical theatre singing must be more direct, accessible in the sense of portraying reality, and able to portray greater dramatic contrast using both broad and subtle strokes. You need not always sound beautiful if you are singing musical theatre, and that doesn't mean that you will be hurting your voice either. There are techniques to making 'ugly' sounds that are quite safe. This book is intended to give a well-rounded picture of the sort of training required for an actor and musical theatre singer. I mention the two in one breath because it is now widely recognised that all actors need to learn to sing; we also require our musical theatre singers to act.

I cannot claim that what is in this book is the whole story of how to sing in the theatre. However, it will provide some sort of template for those of us working in this field who must respond to the changing needs of a theatre environment. Actors are often vulnerable in that they will try to do whatever is asked of them. This book seeks to fill the need that is often opened up in that situation: how do you make the sounds required by the director, your character, the musical director, the style of the music and so on? The book also sets out a method for training that will prepare you to meet those needs.

How to use this book

The book is divided into three sections dealing with fundamental principles, voice training, and the requirements for performance. You need to read and understand Section 1 before you attempt to go any further with the book. Section 2 takes you step-by-step through the process of setting up your voice, and it is based on the principles put forward in Section 1. If you are an experienced actor or singer, it might be possible for you to read Section 1 and then go straight to Section 3. If you then come across something that you do not understand or cannot do, you can always back-track to the appropriate chapter in Section 2.

Sometimes when I am working with an actor I can sense their impatience to get going on a song. I want to emphasise that the process of setting up your voice that makes up Section 2 can run alongside any performing work you are doing. You do not have to stop singing until you get it all 'right'.

You can use Section 2 for trouble-shooting as well. Each chapter deals with a specific aspect of vocalising that you can target if you feel you need work in that area. Certain terms appear over and again, and I suggest you become familiar with them as they are good shorthand for understanding what is happening in your voice. Effort is a key word – it means having an awareness of how hard you are working and where. Singing is a complex activity using many groups of muscles at the same time, and you need to know that your different efforts add up to make the sound you want. Another personal favourite is 'set-up' as in vocal set-up: you can change and adjust your vocal set-up just as you can re-programme a computer. If you don't know how to run your programme or set it up properly, it will go into default. It is the same with your voice; it will only work well for you if you give it the right commands.

Do you need a teacher to work through this book? Not necessarily. Certainly you can do Section 1 on your own. I would like to think that teachers of actors and musical directors will read this book too, that it will inform them in what they are already doing, and that it will be helpful in building a language for talking about singing that is not purely subjective. Since it is not easy for us to hear ourselves when we are singing (to say nothing of mind-sets that we have about how 'good' or 'bad' our voice is), it is useful to have an outside ear to give us a more reliable feedback. I always insist that my students tape their singing lessons for this reason. I recommend that you use a tape recorder often when working the exercises in Sections 2 and 3, and that you do some of the song assignments with a friend so that you can listen to each other. Many actors have a trusted pianist or vocal coach who helps them prepare for auditions. Get your vocal coach in on what you are doing!

It is possible to damage your voice when you are trying out new techniques and do not know what you are doing. Some of the techniques I have described in the book require considerable expertise. Belting is a case in point. Make sure you practise the high-energy voice work as detailed in the book and pay attention if your voice tells you that 'something hurts'. Sometimes we may ache when we start to use muscles that are not worked, but it should never hurt.

How the Voice Works

Chapters 1–4 deal with the nature of the vocal instrument. For centuries singers have been the only instrumentalists who had to guess at how their instrument was working. As science has advanced and scientific instruments have become more sophisticated (and smaller), we have been able to discover more about the voice.

There is a lot of information contained in these chapters. You will not need to remember it all, but you should understand the basic concepts. I think anyone who is interested in singing should have this information – it de-mystifies the act of singing. The artistry of the performer is not diminished by this, but there is a chance that more performers will be better artists because of it. If you want to keep singing a mystery, then this book is probably not for you!

My aim has been to present the information about the vocal instrument as clearly as possible, and in a user-friendly manner. Many of the exercises in these first chapters are about developing awareness. Do not miss them out. Often singing training starts too far along the line and does not address the basics. This means that actors who might otherwise stand a good chance of singing well miss out on the process altogether, and that those with an easier facility do not always acquire a really solid technique.

You'll notice that I do not address breathing until Chapter 4, which is at the end of this section. I do not think that breathing is as important as we have been led to believe in traditional singing training. I feel that to concentrate on breathing to the exclusion of the other functions of the vocal instrument, particularly those of the larynx, is a mistake. So that is why I have started where the voice starts – working with the larynx.

I think that a basic understanding of phonetics is important for singers. When you get to the chapters discussing vowel placement and diction (Chapters 8 and 11), you will see why. Not everyone is familiar with (or likes!) phonetics. Whenever I have used them, I have added an interpretative spelling alongside so that you do not have to interrupt your reading. You should also refer to the vowel and consonant keys on pages 45-47. Because there are differences in pronunciation of certain sounds between American and British English (e.g. 'word'), you should always check the key if in doubt. I have included standard British and standard

American in all the vowel charts.

Finally, some of you may be wondering if, in spite of all the information you are about to acquire, you really *can* learn to sing from a book. I think you can learn a lot. In the old days we learned singing by imitating the teacher, or by trying to make the ideal sound that the teacher had in their head. If you want to work through this book with a teacher or with a friend, I'm sure you will find it useful for the simple reason that it is difficult to hear yourself while you are singing. However, my aim is that, by working with this book, you will start your singing with your own idea of the sound you want to make. It's a more powerful way to begin.

Chapter 1

How do I make the notes?

Recently I gave a first lesson to a bright, intelligent, professional actress who had trained for three years at a Drama College. 'I really don't know how to sing,' she told me. 'I think I've got a voice and I can read music, but I don't know how to make the notes.'

So how do you make the notes? This is where practical physiology is a necessity. You cannot see inside your instrument (unless you pay a visit to the laryngologist) and you do need to know what's going on 'in there'.

In this chapter we shall be looking at the nature of the vocal instrument: it's physical and acoustic properties and what they mean for the singer who plays the instrument. The topics for discussion will include the tube of the vocal tract, the larynx and the vocal folds. There are awareness exercises to put you in touch with the different parts of the mechanism so that you can feel as well as understand what I am talking about.

You will need this information if you are going to use your voice professionally. As an actor or training actor you learn to use your body as a tool – a vehicle for expression – and this learning is a discipline. Similarly with singing: once you have understood how the voice works, you are less likely to be confused by imagery that is unhelpful or by folk-lore about the act of singing, and you will be able to produce the sounds you want. This is true for performers in any musical genre: there is a technique to singing for *Les Misérables* as there is for *Rent* or *Oklahoma!*; and there are techniques for singing like Elton John, Celine Dion and Tina Turner.

THE VOCAL MECHANISM

The vocal tract

Your voice, or vocal tract, is a kind of pipe. At the bottom end, inside the neck, it is relatively narrow. At the top end it opens out inside the mouth and nasal cavity. Look at Diagram 1 overleaf.

The whole vocal tract is a resonator. You can test this by holding your breath and flicking your finger against the side of your neck near the larynx. The sound will be hollow. If you then mouth vowel sounds you can hear how the vocal tract shapes itself differently for each one, even without you introducing any voicing.

The larynx and vocal folds

The larynx is at the top of the windpipe, and forms the housing of the vocal folds. This is where the sound is actually made. The larynx is a vibrator. This is important because a resonator on its own cannot generate the sound, only amplify and shape it. Just as some wind instruments have a reed, your voice has two vocal folds which produce vibrations. This happens when they close against the breath to make sound. Please pay attention to the word 'closed': your vocal folds close and open when you make sound. It's difficult to be aware of your vocal folds vibrating, but you can get a sense of how they work to produce the sound by doing the following awareness exercise.

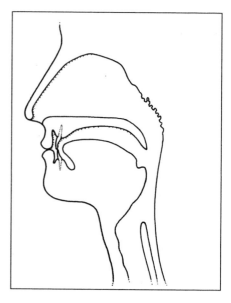

Diagram 1: the vocal mechanism

Awareness exercise 1: THE VIBRATING MECHANISM

1. Blow breath gently through your lips; they should be almost closed. You will get a rather airy sound without pitch.
2. Start to blow a little harder and regulate the pressure until you produce a 'lip trill'. This is not very different from the sound signal produced by the vocal folds at the level of the larynx before it is shaped by the resonator. Notice what you needed for this task:
   i. You needed breath to excite the vibration of the lips;
   ii. You needed to regulate the breath pressure for efficient vibrations – in singing and speaking we call this sub-glottic pressure;
   iii. You needed something that could vibrate: the lips or vocal folds.

   Now see what happens if we introduce vibrations at the larynx and use the vocal tract as a sound shaper.
3. Make the lip-trill again. This time, introduce voice as you do it.

Notice that for this task, you are vibrating at the larynx and at the lips, and that the vocal tract shapes the sound.

MAKING THE NOTES

For good singing, you need airflow (without breath you cannot get vibrations), vocal fold closure, and effective use of the resonators. In addition you will need a support system for your airflow. Here is a diagram to demonstrate this:

Function of the instrument:	**Power**	**Source**	**Filter**
Where it happens:	Lungs	Larynx	Vocal tract
Singing terminology:	Breath	Tone	Resonance

It's important that you grasp that these three components are necessary for vocalisation:

1. the power generated by breath from the lungs;
2. the sound source creating the tone made in the larynx;
3. the filter that can shape and amplify the sound or resonance, which takes place in the vocal tract.

Later we will look at these structures and the muscle groups involved. In the meantime, look at Diagram 2 overleaf of the vocal tract. The power, source and filter areas are indicated.

And how do you make the notes? I'm coming back to that. Very simply, each note or pitch that you make has a specific frequency, or number of vibrations. If you strum or pluck a stringed instrument, you can actually see the string vibrating. When the vocal folds vibrate, they close and open together a set number of times per second according to the note we are singing. The note or pitch we are singing is measured scientifically by the number of vibrations per second (Hertz). This measurement is known as frequency. Look at the example frequencies in relation to music, given below.

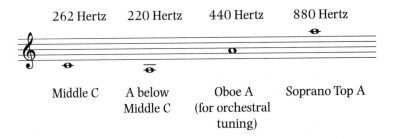

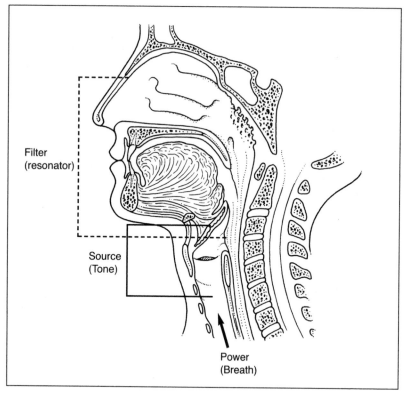

Diagram 2: the vocal tract; breath, tone and resonator

This all happens within the time-span of one second, so your vocal folds are closing and opening 262 times per second on a middle C! And what happens? Well, as you breathe out, a stream of air hits the closed vocal folds and is chopped up into smaller puffs of air. A train of these small puffs of air pressure is what makes up the sound source. In the larynx, where the sound starts, the noise produced is rather like a duck's quack! It is then picked up by the vocal tract and amplified. In the rest of the vocal tract it is modified by the resonating qualities of the tube. So not only do your vocal folds vibrate hundreds of times a second, you also have a personal 'graphic equaliser' in there!

Depending on how you shape your resonators (and this includes what we do with vowels and consonants), you can change the quality of sound you produce. This is what we mean by filtering the sound. There is space behind and around the larynx to resonate (called the laryngo-pharynx), space above in the mouth (oro-pharynx), and also in the nose (naso-pharynx). Bringing your vocal folds together with more or less energy will also alter the sound. We will explore this in Chapters 3 and 7.

'Head' and 'chest' voice: the myth

You may be looking at the power-source-filter diagram and wondering about head and chest voice: these are terms that I do not use except in relation to a student's previous training. They are ancient terms relating to physical sensations and do not give a clear picture of what is happening when we sing. Bear with me as I explain why.

Usually when people are talking about head and chest voice, they are referring to head and chest resonance. Space and air is required for resonance to take place. However, there isn't space and air inside the head anywhere above the nasal cavity except in the sinuses. Now look at the boundaries for each of the cavities in the diagram. You can see that, even if there were space to resonate in the head, there is no way for the sound to get there. So there is no head voice! Now let's consider chest voice. Because you have air in the lungs, the chest *could be* a resonator; however, it is not for the voice because the breath is travelling up through the vocal folds and into the vocal tract. You cannot get resonance from a cavity below the sound source.

What you are feeling is not resonance but vibration. Your whole body is a vibrator; you can feel this if you jump up and down while you are singing. The skeletal frame, which is made up of rigid bone, conducts vibration very well. This is particularly the case with the skull. We get a very strong sensation from bone conduction inside the head. You can feel this if you hum and put your hands over your ears: the hum will sound much louder to you than it does outside. Perhaps the reason why we talk about head resonance is because of the bone conduction. There are also muscles that we use to support the vibrating larynx in singing that are attached to the base of the skull and jaw. This could be another reason for thinking we have a head voice. (We will be looking at these supporting muscles in Chapter 7). So you have one voice and it is located in the larynx. Now let's examine further what happens in the vocal instrument when we make the notes.

The basics of producing the sound

When you sing a note and your vocal folds are vibrating hundreds of times per second, you actually produce a range of frequencies, the strongest of which is the fundamental. We call the note you are singing by this fundamental frequency. The other frequencies are called overtones or harmonics. Let's look at the harmonics which occur with the note C two octaves below middle C.

You'll hear these other harmonics as part of the individual note that is being made. In fact, it's an essential part of what we recognise as 'singing in tune'. Someone who is singing sharp or flat usually isn't resonating properly, so we don't hear all the harmonics we associate with that particular note, and hear it as out-of-tune.

To solve this problem, it is helpful to understand the acoustics of the voice. Acoustics is the science of sound. As an actor you are already aware of acoustics because you know that the space you are working in can alter how you are heard. Understanding a little acoustics helps any instrumentalist, including the vocalist. When an instrumentalist learns to play, he learns how his instrument is put together and is told about its acoustic properties. Often we do not do this in singing teaching, and it leads the student to focus on 'my voice' and whether or not it is 'good enough', and I believe this is unhealthy. A lot of singers forget that we are basically constructed alike, and that the laws of sound are the same for each of us.

Every musical instrument favours certain families of harmonics according to its shape. This is how we can tell the difference between the same note played on different instruments (listen to a violin, a flute, a clarinet and trumpet playing the same note: they all sound different). With the voice, the component parts are the same for each person. That is why we can *all* sing – we all have the 'bits'! However, shapes and sizes of the vocal tract vary as much as our body shapes, so each voice will be unique.

To sum up, here are the basics of producing sound. You need:

1. to create space in the larynx between the true and false vocal folds, so that there is room for the true folds to vibrate and set up harmonics;

2. sufficient breath pressure beneath the vocal folds so that the sound energy is carried to the ears of the listener;

3. to shape your vocal tract so that you can enhance the harmonics that you want to be heard. (This is a matter of choice: if you change the shape of your instrument by making it, say, long or short, wide or narrow, different harmonics will be favoured.)

So that's what happens to make the notes. How you do it is what makes up most of Sections 1 and 2 of this book. You have a wonderful instrument – now learn how to play it.

Practice exercises

A lot of this information may be new to you, so how will you know if you are doing it right when you practise? This can be a problem particularly for those students who are used to getting feedback from their teachers about how they sound. Your teacher is not there when you do your practice, so you need to develop good muscle feedback, or kinaesthetic awareness, for yourself. Part of your training will involve feedback and guidance from a teacher, either in a one-to-one or group situation (both are valuable). However, ultimately you will be doing the singing and for this you need to be self-reliant. Learn to 'listen with your muscles' rather than to your voice, and you will be successful.

Awareness exercise 2: CLOSING THE VOCAL FOLDS

1. Make a sound of friendly caution: 'uh-oh'. The sound should be crisp and not forced. Notice that a small glottal stop precedes each of the vowel sounds.
2. Repeat the sound several times in spoken voice – the feeling is straightforward and easy.
3. Now go to make the sound, but stop just before you do it. Notice that you are holding your breath and that the vocal folds are closed. If you go on to make the sound, the breath will be released through the vocal folds as they start to vibrate.

What can you learn from this? In a purely practical way you can feel that your vocal folds control whether or not the breath passes through and not the other way around. What's more, they need to close in order for you make a sound. This exercise also clarifies that the sound starts not with the breath, not in the chest or the head, but *in the larynx*. This is the closure of the vocal folds that I referred to on page 4 – the sound source. I do not mean to imply that the breath is not involved, but without this closure you will only get a resonance and you won't be able to 'make the notes'.

'Sirening' and the soft palate

Another very important muscle that you need to be in touch with at an early stage is the soft palate. The soft palate is part of your sound filtering mechanism; it can send the sound out through the nose, or through the mouth, or through both at once, so it has a major effect on your resonating quality. The soft palate is not served by many sensory nerve endings and is often difficult to feel, particularly in relation to the tongue and the pharyngeal wall with which it interacts.

Awareness exercise 3: LOCATING THE SOFT PALATE

1. Your palate is touching the back of your tongue when you say 'ng' as in 'sing'. Say 'sing', holding the 'ng' part, and notice that the sound is now coming down your nose. (You'll find more of this later in Chapter 6 which is about controlling the nasal port.)
2. Now gently flick your palate away from the tongue as you say 'ing-ing-ing-ing-ing'. Keep the main part of your tongue in the same position as before.

   Do you feel as if you are opening and closing something as you make this sound? If this didn't give you a feeling for where your palate is, try the following:
3. When you say the consonant 'k', you will be hitting your palate with the tongue. Do the 'k' as hard as you can, noticing that your breath is first held and then released.
4. Now go back and repeat the first exercise with 'ing'.

Let's now explore the vocal mechanism further by sirening.

Awareness exercise 4: THE SIREN

For this exercise, you make a sound imitating the siren of an American-style police car.

1. Begin by putting your tongue and palate together in the 'ng' position, as in the word 'sing'. Your tongue should be raised at the back, and spread at the sides so that it is touching the upper back molars.
2. Start to make very small whining or mewing sounds with your tongue and palate still in this position. The sound will be very quiet and will feel as though it's coming 'from nowhere'. You will need very little breath.
3. Now begin to make a larger excursion with your siren: try a pitch-glide in larger and larger loops like this:

4. Finally, make the siren from the bottom to the top of your vocal range. What do you notice?
i. The siren feels more difficult at certain points in your range (usually at the top and very bottom).
ii. Your voice may 'crack' or disappear at certain points in your range.

Your vocal folds are stretched and are also vibrating faster for the high notes, which means increased work in the larynx. On the lower notes, the vocal fold muscles will relax again and will be vibrating more slowly. Some people have difficulty manoeuvring these changes, leading to an unevenness in the sound. This 'crack' or break in the voice can easily be remedied. Constriction in the larynx can also occur, as a panic reaction to these changes in the vocal folds, causing the voice to cut out completely. Don't worry if this is happening to you now; I'll show you how to fix it in Chapter 5.

For now apply this strategy: make your neck long, and pull up with the back of your head as you siren through those awkward spots in your range. This will have the effect of anchoring your vocal tract as it changes position to accommodate the needs of pitch.

i. Did you feel work in the back of the neck? Or perhaps at the sides around the larynx? Good! You are now experiencing the muscular effort required to maintain pitch.

ii. Did you feel your tongue pushing up against your soft palate at the back of the mouth; maybe even pushing higher for the uppermost pitches? This is all part of the 'work' involved in singing.

By the way, how much breath did you need for Awareness Exercise 4? Not very much. Efficient vocalising is not just about breath. To prove this to yourself repeat Awareness Exercise 4 silently, and notice that you can still feel muscles working. You are now developing awareness; keep 'listening'!

Chapter 2

My voice won't come out at auditions

People often say this to me in a workshop, citing it as a reason for thinking of themselves as non-singers. The thinking seems to be that those to whom 'it' does not happen are blessed with special equipment in the vocal department. Either that, or they have nerves of steel! It would be easy to dismiss this problem as one of nerves, or a lack of self-confidence in the performer, yet it is often quite experienced actors who say it to me. Sometimes we feel more vulnerable when singing than speaking; sustained voicing can be more self revealing. There is a mechanical reason for this particular problem, and it's my experience that if you can deal with the mechanical aspect, it becomes easier to deal with the psychological.

In this chapter we shall be looking at laryngeal constriction and release, and onset of tone. This will enable you to overcome the problem of your voice 'not coming out' in stressful situations. Learning to master the techniques explained here is essential if you want to rely on your voice.

LARYNGEAL CONSTRICTION

If you have experienced your voice seizing up when you get to the audition, or when you have to sing in front of people at all, then there is a perfectly good reason for it. It happens because *the larynx is programmed to constrict!* This may be a bit difficult to grasp if you've been told that singing is 'natural'. It makes sense, however, when you know that the primary function of your larynx is to protect your airways.

What does this mean? It means that the instinctive (natural) functions of the larynx are: to stop food and other foreign substances from going into your lungs, to eject fluid and mucous from the lungs (when we cough), to close up so that you can push and strain in your daily bodily functions, in childbirth, and in straining and lifting. This tendency to close up in the larynx is part of a protective programming that also comes into play when we are under emotional stress or threats such as auditioning, first nights, or even after a row with a significant other.

This is the scenario: it's the morning of your audition or your first performance. You've rehearsed your song, and you know you can do it, but the situation makes you feel nervous and excited. Adrenaline is rushing round your body, your pulse is racing and there are butterflies in your stomach. To the larynx, with its protective programming, this feels like a major threat. So your 'flight or fight' mechanism kicks in and, since you are not going to flunk out of the audition, the larynx prepares to fight and closes down. This is a perfectly natural human response!

The diagrams below show how your vocal folds look from inside and above in two different positions (constricted and wide). Remember that in breathing, the vocal folds are apart and that they come together when we speak or sing. They even come towards each other when we exhale.

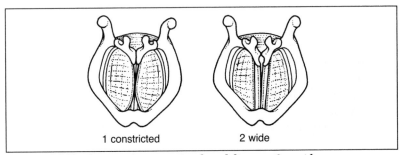

The vocal folds: diagram 1 – constricted, and diagram 2 – wide.

The shaded area on the diagram indicates the position of the false vocal folds. These are the ones that cause all the trouble because, as you see in the Diagram 2, they can close up the airspace above the true vocal folds. This disturbance in the airspace upsets vocal fold vibration. In this way the false vocal folds can either contaminate the sound or stop it from coming out altogether. This is what we mean by 'constriction'.

The false folds are naturally constricted when we are straining or grunting. Try the following exercise.

Awareness exercise 1: CONSTRICTING THE LARYNX

1. From a sitting position, lift your feet off the ground so that they are not supporting any weight.
2. Place both hands under the chair and try to lift you and the chair off the ground. Notice what is happening in the larynx: the false folds will constrict as you work harder to pull yourself up.

What's the sensation? Do you feel something pushing down and inwards at the throat and the air pushing up from underneath at the belly. You are now experiencing constriction.

RETRACTION: THE SILENT LAUGH

What do we do about constriction in order to carry out our task of performing? We can bring into play another human response – laughter! You can overcome constriction by silently laughing in the larynx. Using the posture of laughing in the larynx you can widen the false vocal folds so that the true vocal folds can vibrate freely. This was first discovered by Colton and Brewer in 1974, and was developed into an exercise by Jo Estill.

In the following exercise we widen in the larynx by laughing, while monitoring the effort we make.

Exercise 1: RETRACTION

1. Use your thumbs to create an image of the false vocal folds:
   Thumbs together = constriction;
   Thumbs slightly apart = neutral or relaxed;
   Thumbs wide apart = retraction (or wide space in the larynx).
2. Laugh. Laugh hard rather than loud. Feel the wide space in your larynx.
3. Laugh again, silently. Laugh as hard as you did for stage 2. Notice how hard you are working and give the sensation a number on a scale of one to ten, where one is the least effort you could make to laugh and ten, the most. If you are having difficulty with the idea of silently laughing, think what you would have to do on stage if you found something hilarious but could not let the audience see or hear you were laughing. If you were head miked you would not want to make any sound at all!
4. Now keep the laugh feeling and the effort number that goes with it, and go through the following manoeuvres:
i. Breathe in and out gently and freely.
ii. Chew lazily with your jaw, and roll the tongue around inside your mouth.
iii. 'Wash away' unnecessary tension in your facial muscles.
iv. Walk briskly to reduce body tension and to avoid breath-holding.

Throughout all of this you should maintain your effort number for the silent laugh.

Notice that it is more difficult to remain retracted when other muscles come into play. Remember that your larynx is a valve and is there to protect the airway. The harder we ask our bodies to work, the greater the urge to constrict in the larynx.

Did you get that sense of space that I've been talking about, in your larynx? Did you notice how hard you were working? I'm talking physically here as well as mentally. Did you remember to listen with your muscles? Now repeat Exercise 1, and gently sing a note on the vowel 'EE' when you have reached a retracted position. Don't sing loudly; just notice what you feel.

When I do this exercise with people, they are often surprised at the sounds they can make, particularly the 'non-singers'. A well-trained singer will normally be retracted in the larynx already and recognise the sensation. Actors who have trained in theatre voice, but have sung very little, often need to work at maintaining the retracted position because they are not used to sustaining pitch.

Do you need to do this all the time? Mostly, yes. In everyday speech and relaxed voice qualities, you do not need to be retracted; you simply need to avoid constriction. For projected singing and high-energy voice qualities such as opera and belting, retraction is a must. You should perform Exercise 1 a few times until you can feel for yourself where the constriction is made and released. The technique of retraction (silently laughing) is something you will need when we get to Chapter 5 and start to work systematically at your voice.

In singing, you need to be retracted most of the time. You realise by now that your larynx is a constricting mechanism – a valve – that responds to stressful situations by closing up. Unfortunately the act of singing tends to trigger constriction as well. Singing is effortful: it involves hundreds of vibrations per second in the vocal folds; it involves active use of muscles we use in straining and pushing for 'active expiration'; and it requires us to do something pretty unnatural with our breathing pattern. Besides all this, changes in the larynx which happen in the course of singing an average song – raising and lowering the larynx, shifting the palate, movement in the laryngeal cartilages – all of these may also trigger the larynx to constrict.

The act of singing, however natural our desire to express ourselves through the medium of music, requires a lot of muscular effort. In addition to this, you require good vocal fold vibration. To achieve these 'good vibrations', you need to widen the false vocal folds in the larynx. It's an essential part of good vocalising.

ONSET OF TONE

As we start to sing, the vocal folds need to come together; this is what we mean by onset of tone. You have learned how to deal with constriction in the larynx, and now you need to know how to start the sound. The vocal folds close against the breath (as I mentioned in Chapter 1), and they can achieve this in different ways.

The glottal and aspirate onsets

The glottal onset is made by closing the glottis (the space between the vocal folds) *before* making the tone. So the vocal folds close first, and then the breath comes through as the folds start to vibrate. The opposite happens with an aspirate onset. As its name suggests, the tone in an aspirate onset is initiated by an 'h'; in this case the breath passes through the vocal folds first, and the tone comes second.

You've already experienced a glottal onset in the exercises for awareness at the end of Chapter 1. Let's take it a stage further.

Awareness exercise 2: THE GLOTTAL ONSET

1. Repeat the simple 'uh-oh' in spoken voice. Check that you are retracted when you do this so that there's no danger of constriction.
2. Now go to make the sound again, but stop just before you actually make the sound. The breath will be held by the true vocal folds.
3. Keeping your folds together say 'EE' as you release into the sound. Notice that at the same time, you'll let the breath come through as well.
4. Say 'EE' a few times like this and then start to pitch it on a note in a comfortable part of your voice.
5. Repeat with all the vowels. Notice that there will be a distinct 'edge' at the start of each note and that the breath stops each time before you make the sound.

Compare this with the second type of onset – the aspirate onset.

Awareness exercise 3: THE ASPIRATE ONSET

1. Bring your hand close up to your mouth.
2. Keeping the retracted position in the larynx, blow air onto your hand as you say 'h-OO'. Use plenty of air to build up pressure to the onset.

Notice that you can feel the air on your hand before you make the sound, and much less while you are making it. You won't feel much in the larynx, but you will feel work in the abdominal wall as you blow the breath out.

Repeat the glottal and aspirate onsets with all the vowels. What do you notice about the difference between these two types of onset? Notice the sensation.

With the glottal onset there is a stop before the sound, and you can feel the sound starting in the larynx. With the aspirate onset there is no stop, and you can feel the sound starting on the breath. Both onsets are made in the larynx, of course, but the sensations are quite different. Neither one of them is wrong. They sound different too. The glottal onset gives a sharper, speech-like quality; the aspirate gives a breathy quality.

Now the glottal onset, as you may know, tends to get a bad press! This is because we want to avoid too much pressure on the true vocal folds and, of course, constriction. A lot of people who have hoarse voices press the vocal folds together too hard when doing the glottal onset. You've already discovered that it can be done with a minimum of effort and no constriction. You are going to need this onset as it can be used to eliminate breathy tone, to help you find the thickness needed in your folds to make bottom notes, for clear diction, and to stress words.

Conversely, when you performed the aspirate onset, you sang 'on the breath'. You need to know how that feels too, and you might use it if you are one of those people with 'pressed phonation' and a hoarse voice. (Please note that I'm not suggesting that pressed phonation and glottal onsets are the only causes of hoarseness.)

Aspirate gradual

You can also perform a more gradual version of the aspirate onset by simply blowing the air more gently and slowly. If you control the outflow of air from the abdomen, you can initiate the tone without a pop at all. This will give you a sensation of really coasting on the breath, and will produce a quieter sound than the usual aspirate, which requires a build-up of air to bring the folds together. You may find this type of aspirate onset useful for very quiet singing if you are close-miked, or singing ensemble.

Simultaneous onset

The third type of onset is often know as the 'singer's onset' or the 'glide onset'. It's also called the simultaneous onset because the breath and the tone seem to start together. Simply described, it differs from the other two onsets in that there's neither a glottal stop nor an aspirate 'h' before the sound. It's something in-between and requires quite a lot of control.

Because this onset requires a change in the larynx we need to consider what we mean by 'effort' before going any further. When I talk about effort in the book, I am asking you to have awareness of what you are doing when you are working with your voice. This awareness of effort is absolutely essential for good and safe singing. You need to:

1. Know how hard you are working;
2. Isolate the muscles used in tasks;
3. Monitor the spread of effort and decide whether it is appropriate to the task.

In Exercise 1 for retracting the larynx, you carried out a task-based exercise. You consciously used your false vocal folds to constrict in the larynx and then to retract. The result was a more open sound. Any physical task in the body requires a degree of effort. This does not mean strain or tension, but simply that you are working. What's important is that you can organise yourself to use muscles – or groups of muscles – appropriately for any given task.

When you have ascertained where you are working in the body, you can go through the following list of manoeuvres – the Isolation Checklist – to relax the muscles you do not need for the task. Monitoring effort means that you hold or maintain effort in the muscles or groups of muscles that you need to be working, and then *systematically release the others* to eliminate unnecessary tensions in the vocal mechanism and in the body.

ISOLATION CHECKLIST

Release the abdominal wall so that you can breathe in and out easily (if in doubt walk about briskly)
Silently laugh at the larynx
Chew freely with the jaw
Roll the tongue around inside the mouth
Speak softly on vowel sounds and/or siren through your range.
(For this last stage you learn to hold effort in the body or larger muscles in the vocal tract without transferring it to the vocal folds.)

With this new strategy for monitoring of effort in mind, you can now proceed with work on the simultaneous onset. This onset is very much associated with classical singing and the sensation of 'drinking in with the breath', which is so much talked about. When you do this onset the sense of preparation is different, and there is a small initiating sound before the vowel.

Awareness exercise 4: THE SIMULTANEOUS ONSET

1. Silently laugh to retract the false vocal folds.
2. Prepare the larynx by quietly whining or crying like a small child; there will be a change of posture in the larynx.
3. Hold this posture and the silent laugh. Then using hardly any breath, say 'EE', very gently and quietly.
4. Repeat the sequence and say 'EE' three times, putting a space between each one. Notice what is happening with the breath: it appears to stand still as you start the note.

If you did this correctly you will have made a simultaneous onset with the breath and the tone starting together. You may have been surprised at how little breath was needed to make this onset and at how much effort there was in muscles in the larynx. As you made the preparation for sound, you may have felt as though you made a tiny whimper before the sung tone. This is OK; it is felt rather than heard. This is a difficult onset requiring vocal control, so don't worry if you couldn't do it at this stage; you really need to acquire a bit more knowledge and laryngeal awareness before you can do it with confidence.

Controlling the start of a sound is tremendously important, so I recommend that you practise the three types of onset described above, until you can feel and hear the differences between them. Later on in the book, you will be applying the onsets as part of learning more advanced techniques.

Chapter 3

But I thought I wasn't supposed to feel anything!

This chapter will include easily understandable information on how to feel and locate the parts of the larynx. There will be reference to some of the information given in Chapter 1. The awareness exercises used will form a basis for technical skills you will be learning later on in the book.

It is interesting that training actors who spend much time working with their bodies, developing physical and vocal awareness, often have no sense of their larynx. Singers are sometimes worse: they keep the whole thing shrouded in mystery and tend to develop dependency on their teachers. Despite the advances of scientific knowledge, we seem to have had a Victorian attitude towards our larynx, as though it is wrong to feel anything 'down there'! There has also been a belief that we have no conscious control over the muscles of the larynx and therefore it is better to leave well alone.

You need to know your instrument. A young singer-songwriter was sent to me by his previous teacher because he had started to have difficulties with his singing and kept losing his voice. When I asked him what he thought was the problem, he said, 'It's because I have air trapped in my throat.' I puzzled over this because he was quite definite about it, even though I knew what he described could not actually be happening. Eventually, as I worked through my checklist of the vocal mechanism, I identified the reason for his sensation of trapped air: he had no control over his nasal port and was feeling the change in airflow as air passed from the nasal cavity to the oral cavity at the back of the pharynx. He had no feedback to tell him the difference between his nose and his mouth: to him it was all 'throat'. There was, in fact, nothing wrong with his voice, but because of his nasal port problem he was pushing air all the time and getting tired.

Singers and professional voice users may experience difficulty in getting in touch with their larynx because the reflex actions of swallowing and protection of the airways are so powerful that they tend to mask all other sensations. The larynx is there to protect your airways: to rise, to constrict and close up so that foreign matter cannot get into the breathing system. If foreign matter does get past the larynx, it's quickly and forcibly ejected. The pharynx, which roughly speaking forms the back wall of vocal tract (as well as the oral and nasal cavities), is mostly engaged in getting the food where it needs to be: down the oesophagus. In fact, almost all the muscles used in singing and speaking – the jaw, the tongue, the palate, the muscles of the pharynx and larynx – are exercised on a daily basis though the simple act of feeding. Let's look at what happens when we eat and swallow food:

1. We use the jaw and a range of related muscles to chew the food.

2. The tongue, at the alveolar ridge, pushes the food upwards into the hard palate and backwards towards the pharyngeal wall.

3. In the meantime the soft palate closes up to stop the food going down your nose!

4. Strong muscular impulses from the muscles of the pharynx send the food down to a sphincter muscle at the top of the oesophagus, which then opens up to let the food in.

5. Meanwhile, your larynx kicks into action to make sure that none of the food gets into the windpipe.

6. Once the palate has closed the larynx rises, the epiglottis folds down, and the true and false vocal folds make a strong seal in a sphincter-like action that protects the airways.

I hope you find this as fascinating as I do! What is amazing is that the list of structures and their actions I have just described could act as an index for the act of singing. Obviously the business of feeding and breathing are life-important, and it's essential that these things can take place as reflex or autonomic actions.

LARYNGEAL ORIENTEERING: A SHORT COURSE

It is difficult to feel what is happening in the larynx when you sing. But you can, and it doesn't take long to develop a feedback you can rely on and use as a basis for training muscles to do what you want. Let's start by considering how we can develop awareness of the larynx.

Awareness exercise 1: GENERAL AWARENESS

Think about a part of your body – say – your big toe. How do you know it is there? Can you feel it just by putting your attention on it, or do you need to look at it? Or move it? Probably you wriggled your toe inside your shoe or sock in order to check that it was there. But if there had been no shoe or sock, and if you hadn't moved the big toe, how did you know it was actually there?

So how do you feel your larynx? When are you aware of it? (Incidentally, a large part of the brain is assigned to the big toes as they enable us to walk and to balance, so this was an easier task than feeling the larynx.) There are three ways to feel the larynx:

1. by swallowing (as it moves);
2. by vocalising (you will feel it when it vibrates);
3. by feeling it from outside by touch.

Let's explore the last possibility further.

Feeling the larynx, 'hands on'

A lot of people are wary of touching the larynx and I would certainly agree that, unless you are in the hands of professional such a speech therapist, an osteopath or an ENT surgeon, it is only advisable to do this yourself. Most people feel very vulnerable around the area of the larynx because it is to do with our airways and how we 'give voice' to our feelings. However, I encourage all my students to self-monitor by feeling their own larynx.

Awareness exercise 2: FEELING THE LARYNX

1. Start by locating the base of your tongue. Feel with both thumbs underneath your chin and swallow. You will notice that the tongue performs a strong 'kicking' movement as part of the swallow.
2. Now gently put your thumb and one finger around the first bit of bone you can feel just below the base of the tongue. This will be the hyoid bone which is considered to be the top of the larynx. It's not attached to the spine so it may feel a bit wobbly. If you jut your chin forwards a little, it will be easier to feel the hyoid bone, which is shaped like a horse-shoe.
3. Swallow again and notice that the hyoid bone will move both up and forwards.
4. Now gently walk your thumb and finger down a little at the front. You will go through a dip and come to another structure. This one is cartilage, not bone. It has a texture like gristle – don't let that alarm you. You have almost certainly found your thyroid cartilage, which forms part of the housing for the vocal folds. It's shaped like a shield and has a notch in the front. In men, the notch is more prominent and is known as the Adam's apple. Notice that the thyroid goes quite wide around the sides – it is open, in fact, at the back.
5. Below the thyroid is the cricoid cartilage. It is shaped like a signet ring (with the large part at the back) and sits on top of your windpipe. You may feel a very small dip again, between it and the thyroid above. The cricoid and the thyroid together house the vocal folds, and are generally what people mean when they talk about the larynx.

If you look at the following diagram of the laryngeal cartilages it might help you to visualise what you are feeling.

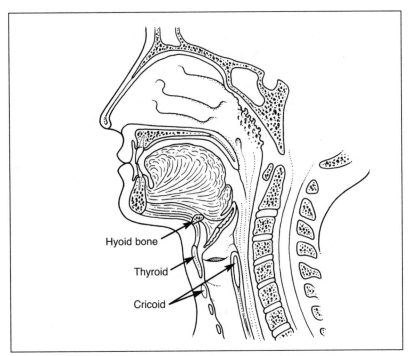

Diagram 1: the thyroid and cricoid cartilages

Moving the larynx

Now that you have some idea of how to feel what is there in the larynx, here are a few guidelines for gaining awareness of how it moves. Don't try to feel it from outside to begin with; just perform the movements.

Awareness exercise 3: RAISING AND LOWERING YOUR LARYNX

1. Raise your larynx by making a small squeak or siren on a high pitch. The larynx naturally rises with high pitches.
2. Lower your larynx by doing a 'yawn-sigh' manoeuvre. Start off on a yawn and sigh out as you finish. Most people breathe in deeply as they yawn and this will tend to lower the larynx from a pull on the connective tissue between the larynx and the windpipe.

Awareness exercise 4: MOVING THE LARYNX FORWARDS AND BACKWARDS

1. Assume the posture of someone about to whine or whimper. The thyroid cartilage of the larynx will move forwards.
2. Now start to swallow, stopping near the beginning of your swallow as though something is stuck on its way down. Your larynx will move a little way backwards.

What I've described is the range of movement that can be expected from a healthy larynx in everyday functioning. Go through the movements again while feeling the larynx from the outside with your thumb and two fingers. Don't worry if the movements are small; they are subtle.

We are doing this because I want to demonstrate to you that you can feel things in the larynx and that it is OK to do so while singing. Also, there are a number of things that you will be learning in this book that require you to move structures in the larynx. Generally, I have found that the only awareness of laryngeal movement taught in vocal training is that of lowering. Lowering the larynx takes considerable muscular effort since the larynx is geared to rise up as part of our swallowing reflex. Perhaps this is why we feel it more, but lowering is by no means the only, nor the most important, movement we can feel in the larynx.

In the exercises I use for developing range and dealing with so-called breaks in the voice, particularly in sirening, you will need to know whether or not your larynx is raising, lowering, or just being where it naturally 'sits'. (This last is a neutral position.) Raising the larynx is essential for easy access to the highest pitches. In the soprano and tenor voice, if you do not allow the larynx to rise on the notes around the upper E or F area, you may hit a break or crack in the range. In singing teaching, this problem is sometimes referred to as the second passaggio. If you are a mezzo or baritone voice, you may well experience the second passaggio two or three notes earlier in your range. Notice this change in the larynx when you practise the siren; if you lower the larynx as you approach these notes in your range (mistakenly trying to make more space for the high notes), you will run into difficulties.

When you practise the siren, make a note of when you change laryngeal height; there is a neutral, a high and a low position for the larynx, as well as all the gradations in-between. What is important is to have a good range of movement and not to 'fix' the larynx in one place.

By raising and lowering the larynx we can also alter the length of the vocal tract tube. This will change your resonating quality. The deeper tones of a lowered larynx are preferred by some schools of teaching and are desirable as part of the set-up for the operatic voice. However, this is an aesthetic consideration, not one of vocal health; it is not necessary to lower the larynx for healthy voicing. A high larynx is essential for some of the voice qualities currently used in musical theatre – notably twang and belt. By learning to raise and lower your larynx, you have a *choice* and can adjust according to the sort of sound you want to make, where you are in your vocal range, and according to the acoustic space you are working in.

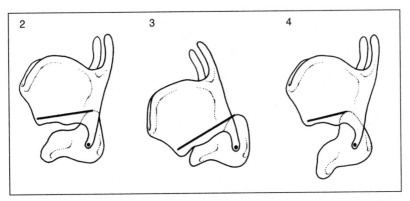

The thyroid and cricoid cartilages: diagram 2 – neutral position, diagram 3 – forward tilt of thyroid cartilage, and diagram 4 – forward tilt of the cricoid cartilage

Changing posture in the larynx

The very notion of a 'posture' in the larynx may be new to you. Yet you are probably familiar with the idea of 'stacking your body' correctly to achieve a balanced standing posture. Since we can move the parts of the larynx, we have a number of postures available to us.

Look at Diagrams 2-4 of the thyroid and cricoid cartilages and notice that there are three possible positions.

1. *Neutral.* This is where the larynx should be 'at rest' and for everyday speaking.

2. *Forward tilt of the thyroid cartilage.* This position enables the vocal folds to be stretched longer and thinner for higher pitches. You will have difficulty accessing your upper range if you do not do this forward tilting. Using this tilt will also help you to access vibrato and sweetness in your sound.

3. *Forward tilt of the cricoid cartilage.* This position in the larynx is required for safe belting. You are most likely to access it if you do not breathe deeply, but take a breath into the upper chest.

Awareness exercise 5: TILTING THE THYROID:

1. Make a small mewing sound like a tiny kitten: 'miaow'. If this doesn't work for you, whine like a small child or a puppy. The sound has to be a high(ish) in pitch, but don't try to sing. Just make the noise. Most people can do this after a little practice.
2. Make sure you are retracted so that you can avoid constriction. You are now doing the thyroid tilt.

Compare this with your neutral position. Do the glottal onset from Chapter 2 on a low pitch, then go back to the miaow or whine. Notice that the sensations are very different.

Awareness exercise 6: TILTING THE CRICOID:

You are going to take an upper chest breath.

1. Put a hand on your breastbone and feel the breath coming into the chest as you gasp in surprise. (This will also help you to raise the larynx.)
2. Make a small squeak on the vowel 'EE' keeping the silent laugh at all times. The sound should not be loud.

Probably you have tilted the cricoid in this manoeuvre. This type of tilting is difficult to isolate, but you need to know that it exists and that it is a necessary part of the set-up for safe belting. We shall look at tilting the cricoid in more detail in Chapter 12.

Don't worry that I have asked you to do two things which are normally considered to be 'bad' in singing, i.e. taking an upper chest breath and making a squeak. The voice is capable of many things, and both these actions can be performed safely if you have awareness and are able to retract the false vocal folds.

Posture and the larynx

The inexperienced singer will often change posture in the neck in order to achieve extremes of the range. It is difficult to feel 'high' and 'low' and so we tend to try to do it from the outside. Some singers will put their chins down to get low notes and lift up to get the high ones. Remind yourself that pitch is made in the larynx and that you can aid this process by keeping your head and neck in alignment.

For the thyroid tilt (which you do need for the high notes), you will find it helpful to actively elongate the back of the neck by pushing up and back from the base of the skull. This will enable the muscles at the back of the pharynx to support the tilting of the thyroid. I think this work we feel in the back of the neck as we prepare for the high notes may be a reason for talking about 'head voice'.

When tilting the cricoid, the postural work is slightly more complex. I have mentioned that it is not good to poke the chin forward in order to get the high notes. Yet quite often in belting you will see singers with the head back and chin lifted up slightly. This change of posture certainly seems to make the cricoid tilting (essential in belting) easier. However, it's no good if the back of the neck is collapsed as you do this, and in order to avoid collapsing you will need to brace your body further down in the back so

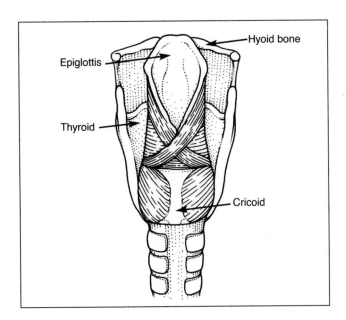

Diagram 5:
rear view of
larynx

that you can support this unusual posture. I will discuss this in more detail as we come to belting in Chapter 12.

There is one more structure in the larynx which I should mention here although I will not be giving you any exercises to feel it. This is the epiglottis, another piece of cartilage, which folds down over the larynx when we swallow. If you look at Diagram 5, you will see that it is shaped like a curled leaf. In effect, there is ring of muscle around it going to the arytenoid cartilage, which can tighten up and narrow the top of the laryngeal tube. This produces the sound quality known as 'twang'.

If Chapter 1 was about the components of vocalising, introducing the structures involved and how they work, this one has been about how the structures move (the physiology) and what it feels like. This kinaesthetic awareness of how-we-do-what-we-do is essential to singers. Without it, we cannot rely on our voices and can never truly be confident.

Chapter 4

What exactly is support?

'Good voice, but not enough support.' This is a frequently-heard critique of someone's singing. What exactly does it mean? By 'support' people can mean either airflow and breath management, or using the body to assist work in the larynx. These two are not the same; it is possible to use both together, but it is important not to confuse them functionally. Body work is not breath use, and working with the breath will not necessarily support work in the larynx. In this chapter I shall be dealing with airflow and breath management. In Chapter 7 we will learn how to engage the body to assist the work done by the larynx and vocal folds.

PASSIVE RESPIRATION

Let's start by looking at what happens when we breathe normally, which is something you have been doing all your life! This is quiet or passive respiration. We breathe in as a response to signals from the brain. The trigger for the signal is the need for oxygen. On receiving the signal the diaphragm contracts and pulls down, decreasing the air pressure in the chest so that the lungs fill with air. Other muscles also help by expanding the chest cavity; these are the muscles that raise the ribs and increase the width and depth of the ribcage. The diaphragm, however, is responsible for 60-80% of the work during inspiration.

When we breathe out, the diaphragm relaxes back to its normal, dome-like position, the chest cavity decreases, and air leaves the body. This is all that needs to happen during quiet respiration, and it happens automatically. Please note that the diaphragm is not active in expiration, so you do not support with or from the diaphragm. Also, you cannot feel the diaphragm, only the effects of it contracting and drawing the air into the lungs.

When you breathe in, you will feel that your lower abdomen moves out as a result of the diaphragm pulling down. You will also feel the 5th to 12th ribs raising and the back expanding just where the ribcage ends. This is because the diaphragm is attached to the lower ribs and to the spine. All this happens automatically if you do not interfere with the functioning of the diaphragm. You need make no conscious effort to lift your ribs in order to draw air into the lungs.

When you breathe out, the space in your chest will decrease and your abdomen and ribs will return to their normal position.

It is a standard part of training for many actors to do floor work enabling them to get in touch with this totally natural process, which will happen very easily if we don't interfere with it. However, it is not the same when we are singing (nor when using projected speaking voice), because we are doing something fundamentally 'unnatural' in singing that requires a different awareness and a more energetic use of the body.

ACTIVE EXPIRATION

In singing we need to sustain pitch – it's the fundamental thing that differentiates speech from song. In order to maintain pitch we need controlled and sustained vocal fold vibration. Some styles of singing require less sustaining power, but the necessity to maintain pitch is common to all styles and to all voice qualities. This requires airflow and balanced air pressure.

Relatively little research has been done on the muscles of expiration for singing, and what there is concludes that different singers use different methods successfully. So why do we talk about breathing so much in singing teaching? Maybe it is because we can see and feel the breathing more easily. What we cannot see (without going to the laryngologist) is the work that the vocal folds are doing in singing to resist the breath. This is fundamental to understanding breath use, and it is too often overlooked.

Chapter 1 dealt with sub-glottic pressure. Sub-glottic pressure is the term used to describe the relationship between the flow of air and the pressure beneath the vocal folds that is required for singing. There are a few key points to note here:

1. The valve mechanism of the vocal folds controls the outflow of air.

2. You must generate airflow for good singing, because the vocal folds require an adequate supply of air to resist.

3. Your airflow needs to be appropriate to the singing task; the airflow and level of vocal fold resistance will differ according to the type of sound you make.

I want to examine these points in a little more detail, also to look at what can interrupt the airflow. Once these points are understood, you will have more information about what can go wrong with breath use and can target the appropriate exercises for dealing with your particular difficulties.

The valve mechanism

It is not the diaphragm, nor the ribs, nor the abdominal wall that controls the outflow of air, but the vocal folds – the valve mechanism. This information may come as a surprise but is nevertheless true. At the top of the chest cavity, which houses the lungs, are the vocal folds, which can close against the breath. You already know this from Awareness exercise 2, Chapter 1, in which we closed the vocal folds. As soon as we start vocalising, the vocal folds will be closing and opening against the breath, allowing it to come through. According to how much resistance is offered by the vocal fold muscles, more or less air will be allowed through.

Awareness exercise 1: REVIEWING ONSET OF TONE

Review the work we did on onset of tone (Chapter 2, pages 15-19).
1. What happens when you do the glottal onset? The breath stops before you make the sound. What stops the breath? Is it the abdomen, or is it the vocal folds? Notice that, if you have closed the vocal folds, it does no good to push upwards from the abdomen unless the vocal folds open to let the breath through and the sound out.
2. Do the aspirate onset. This time, you will notice that the sound does come as a result of the breath being pushed up from the abdomen, and that you can stop the sound if you release the abdomen to breathe in again.
3. Perform the simultaneous onset. Notice that the breath seems to stand still as you start the sound. In fact, it feels as though you are making this tiny sound without breath at all!

Can you feel what is happening? Because something different was happening in the vocal folds, your breath flow changed. That is all I want you to notice.

Generating airflow

Good singing requires airflow. If there is no airflow, there can be no sub-glottic pressure, and, ultimately, no sound. If your airflow is insufficient you will either drive the voice by pressing the vocal folds together (pressed phonation) or make a very small sound because there is not enough airflow to bring the folds together efficiently. In this latter case, the vocal folds will meet only along the free border of the muscle; you hear this sometimes in boy choristers and in the clear but tiny voices of little girls.

There are two factors that give rise to problems with airflow:
1. Breath-holding. This happens when the student does not breathe out enough. You can solve this problem by practising Awareness exercises 5

and 6, (page 37) which feature rolled 'R' and lip trills.

2. **Inefficient in-breath.** This results from holding at the abdomen so that the diaphragm cannot pull down fully. You can solve this problem by working on Exercise 1 (page 34) for elastic recoil.

Appropriate airflow

Airflow needs to be appropriate to the singing task. Thomas Hixon has made one of the most detailed studies of breath use in his book *Respiratory Function in Speech and Song* (1987). He analysed the muscles used in the breath support of opera singers and of actors, and concluded that some singers used abdominal wall support, some used rib reserve, and some a combination of both. All of them used their respective strategies successfully.

The uninterrupted vocal line considered desirable in classical singing is not necessarily a requirement for other styles; a jazz singer, for example, will frequently articulate or accent their phrasing by breaking up the line. In modern musical theatre there is a style of delivering narrative, similar to recitative in opera, that generally requires a speech-like quality (for instance, 'At the end of the day', the opening sequence of *Les Misérables*, or sequences from Sondheim's *Into the Woods*). You do not want uninterrupted line in these instances, and breath use is different in speech quality as we shall discover in Chapter 12. If you are belting you will not use much air because the vocal folds stay closed for longer in belting than in other voice qualities. So this is another instance of noticing that the breath behaves differently in different situations. Here is an awareness exercise demonstrating breath use in different vocal tasks.

Awareness exercise 2: MONITORING AIRFLOW

Monitor your airflow as you do the following:

1. Do an aspirate onset, blowing the breath onto your hand before initiating the tone: 'hEE', 'hEH', 'hAH', and so on. Then hold the note. Pay attention to what is happening in your abdomen. Put your hand over the navel; the abdomen will be working quite hard, going inwards to push the air out.

2. Do a glottal onset, remembering to close the vocal folds before making the tone, and then hold the note. What did you feel this time in the abdominal wall? Much less air going out and possibly, if you held the note for a while, some work around the sides of the abdominal wall. More of this later.

3. Do the simultaneous onset. Remember that you need a tilted posture in the larynx to perform this onset (miaow or whine sensation) and that

the tone is initiated with neither a pop nor an aspirate 'h'. Again, once you have started to sing, hold the note. (If you are having difficulty with the simultaneous onset, try sirening instead. Siren gently and quietly, and settle on one note, holding the pitch as you move from 'ng' [ŋ]to 'EE'.)

What did you notice about your breath use? For the simultaneous onset (or siren), you used hardly any breath to make the sound and were able to hold the note for a long time. Your abdomen moved inwards hardly at all, and you felt more and more work in the body as you held the note longer. These muscles were active in holding the breath back as you sang!

If you were really using awareness in this exercise, you will have noticed a substantial difference in the way the breath behaved in each of these three modes of voicing. This was because it met with different levels of resistance in the vocal folds. Here are two key points that I want you to remember as you work through the rest of this chapter: *the larynx is a valve mechanism, not an open space; good breath management is about airflow and resistance.* You will find these points particularly important when we learn to create different voice qualities in Chapter 12. You cannot create good twang quality if you are pushing air, and you will scratch you voice in belting if you build up too much pressure beneath the vocal folds.

Interruption of airflow in singing

A lot of singing and voice teaching concentrates on the idea of uninterrupted airflow, or sustained and constant air pressure. So there is talk of 'singing on the breath' and 'using a column of air' and other similar images. However, this isn't really what happens, even in classical singing.

Airflow in singing is interrupted:

1. when you onset the tone (unless you are doing an aspirate onset);

2. when you articulate stopped consonants, such as 'p', 't', 'k', and 'b', 'd', 'g';

3. when you articulate fricatives, such as 'f', 'sh' [ʃ], 's', and 'v', 'ge' [ʒ], 'z'. (When making these consonants, you will use up your air very fast.)

You have already discovered that the breath stops momentarily just before you make the sound. This is true unless you are starting with a consonant that is made with the breath: the fricatives 'f', 'sh' [ʃ], 's', and their voiced equivalents, and the nasals 'n', 'm', 'ng' [ŋ], and approximants 'l', 'h'.

Awareness exercise 3: CONSONANTS

1. Articulate the following voiceless fricatives: 'f', 'sh' [ʃ], 's'. Notice what is happening with the breath; they require a lot of air in their production.
2. Sing the voiceless fricatives again and put a vowel after each one. What do you notice? You do not go into voice until after you have articulated the fricative, and you are using up most of your breath up on it. In fact, you probably needed to breathe after each sound.
3. Repeat stages 1 and 2 with these stopped consonants: 't', 'p', 'k'. Monitor your breath use. Again you will observe that you do not come into voice until after you have made the consonant, and that, in the case of these sounds, the breath is stopped before you make them. In addition, because there is a burst of air following the stop, you will find that making these sounds uses up a lot of air.

Did you notice how much effort was involved in making these consonants? Working the consonants is a wonderful way to develop a responsive abdominal wall. And I haven't given you a single breathing exercise yet! What conclusions can you draw from this awareness exercise? Simply that our breath use is not the same all the time; it is not steady and uninterrupted. What you need, in fact, is a flexible and muscular breathing apparatus that will allow the breath to free-vary (work appropriately) according to the vocal task.

Breath management

If you are going to free-vary with the breath, you need some strategies for breath management. The first two exercises that follow address the problem of insufficient airflow. They are followed with work that focuses on the waistband, or muscles of the abdominal wall for maintaining pressure in the chest. These exercises are based on the work of Janice Chapman, and I along with many other teachers and performers, am grateful for the work she has done and generously passed on in this field. I'd also like to acknowledge the work of Meribeth Bunch in explaining the mechanics of these exercises. The following sequence is the single most important breathing exercise you need learn.

The most common breathing problem of singers is not releasing the abdominal wall to breathe in. The diaphragm cannot work efficiently if you lock the abdominal wall. So at all times you must have the capability to breathe reflexively or recoil. You can do this exercise standing, sitting or lying down. Generally I only do floor work with students who do not have good contact with their bodies; I like to get people upright as soon as possible because this is our main working position.

Exercise 1: THE ELASTIC RECOIL.

This exercise comes from the Accent Method.

1. Put one hand over your abdomen. Your thumb should be roughly over your navel.
2. Breathe out sharply on the sound 'PShhh'. Use your hand to send the abdomen right back towards your backbone. Don't bother to breathe in for this – you always have air in your lungs. Just concentrate on this energetic exhalation.
3. Notice that if you wait and allow your abdominal wall to relax at the end of the sound, the abdomen will bounce outwards and you will have breathed in. (For some people this 'bounce back' is actually quite slow to begin with, but it can be done quickly with practice.) Don't panic if this recoil breath didn't happen; as you continue with the exercise it will.
4. Repeat stages 2 and 3 a few times, until you feel that you are getting some movement inwards as you make the sound, and some movement outwards as you breathe in.

When our bodies are balanced and our movements co-ordinated, we are often aware of rhythm taking over. It's the same with the breath. Now work the following exercise.

Exercise 2: WORKING THE RECOIL WITH RHYTHM

1. Work with any or all of these voiceless fricatives: 'f', 'sh' [ʃ], 's'. Make up a sequence with them, and start to build a comfortable rhythm as you breath in and out.
   Here are some example sequences using 'sh' [ʃ]:
   i.   Sh / Sh / Sh; take a breath between each sound;
   ii. sh-Sh / sh-Sh / sh-Sh; the letters in lower case here indicate upbeats; breathe between the pairs of sounds;
   iii. sh-Sh-Sh-Sh / sh-Sh-Sh-Sh; breathe after every four sounds.
   Remember that you breathe out on the sounds, sending your abdomen inwards, and you release your abdominal wall to recoil or breathe in.
2. You can work with these sounds in a variety of ways with different rhythms, using up-beats and as many main beats as you like. (An up-beat is the small beat before the main rhythmic stroke, like the unstressed syllable of the iambic metre.) When you do many repeated sounds on the out-breath, do not worry if your appear to do a part-recoil in-between; it doesn't matter. What is important is that the abdomen is moving inwards on each sound so that you can develop flexibility and muscularity of the abdominal wall.
   The voiceless fricatives help you to feel a build up of pressure against the airflow. However, make sure that you do not grip the jaw or lips as

you make the sounds, as you will be making undue effort and might trigger constriction.

3. Repeats stages 1 and 2 with voiced fricatives: 'v', 'ge' [ʒ], 'z'.

Watch out for the following:

i. Fricatives are made with the breath, and you will feel work at the point of obstruction (lips and tongue);

ii. With voiceless sounds ('f', 'sh' [ʃ], 's'), you should feel nothing in the larynx because the vocal folds are not involved;

iii. With the voiced sounds you will feel more; you are forming the consonants in exactly the same way, but you will feel vibration in the lips ('v'), and tongue ('ge' [ʒ], 'z') and in the larynx.

iv. With all of these voiced sounds you may also feel (and see, if you look in the mirror) your neck pulsating. This is fine; it is just your larynx vibrating as the vocal folds offer resistance to the oncoming air.

This sequence should be practised in short bursts – about five minutes at a time is good – and it can form the beginning of a regular warm up routine. Mastering the recoil breath is fundamental to successful singing. Make sure that you can do the recoil before you try to work the exercises that follow.

Earlier in this chapter, I mentioned that you might feel work around the sides of the abdominal wall, in the waistband area. This is something you will feel as a result of a level of resistance in the vocal folds, particularly in sustained singing. It is a useful way of monitoring the outflow of breath in these circumstances. In this case, you are working with the muscles of the abdominal wall to maintain air pressure in the chest cavity when singing sustained passages of music. You will find it a useful technique when singing a ballad.

Awareness exercise 4: THE WAISTBAND

1. Put your hands around your waistband at the sides; the thumbs should be going into the back of the waistband. Make sure you are working with the fleshy area between the bottom of your ribcage and the top of the pelvic crest. You should not be feeling bone.

2. Cough quite gently. You will feel the muscles of the abdominal wall contract. You will experience this as a jump or push outwards of the muscles at either side of your waistband. The muscles will be contracting around the back, and also further down diagonally into the groin area.

3. Keeping your attention on the same area – the waistband and the muscles going into the groin – now voice a 'v' vigorously. Notice that the muscles will contract or jump outwards as they did in the cough. This will happen even though you are still sending the central section

of your abdominal wall inwards towards the backbone as we were doing earlier to create airflow. The sensation of sending the abdomen inwards will not be as strong as before because you will be feeling a lateral pull as well. This is fine, so long as you know that your airflow is still there.

This mixture of sensations in the abdominal wall is a source of confusion to many students: some believe that any tightening in the abdominal wall will prevent them from using their diaphragm; others believe that support is created by pushing the centre of the abdomen outwards. So the guideline when you are vocalising is that:

1. the navel moves inwards;
2. the waistband moves laterally.

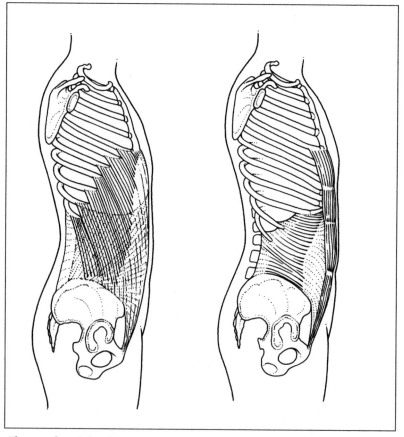

The muscles of the abdominal wall: diagram 1 – the internal and external oblique; diagram 2 – transverse abdominis and rectus abdominis.

This lateral movement of the abdominal wall should not be engaged during inspiration; you should only feel these muscles engage during vocalising. If you try to use them during inspiration you will lock both the body and the breath. Always release the abdominal wall, especially around the navel, when you have finished your phrase and want to breathe in. If you look at Diagrams 1 and 2, you can see the muscles you are feeling for outlined on the body torso.

Awareness exercise 5: THE ABDOMINAL WALL (TOP AND BOTTOM)

There are two other places where you can get feedback from your support muscles: the xyphoid process (the point just underneath your breastbone and where the ribs start to part), and the point just above your pubic arch.

1. Press with your fingers on both these areas. They represent the top and bottom of the abdominis rectus muscle in the abdominal wall.
2. Roll an 'R' vigorously. If you can't roll an 'R', use the lip-trill instead. As the abdominis muscle contracts, you will feel it pushing out under your fingers. (You are still sending the area just below your navel towards your backbone to create airflow.)
3. Roll an 'R' or lip-trill up and down through your range; don't sing, just vocalise. Notice the feedback you get from these two points as you are vocalising.

Awareness exercise 6: THE DIAMOND

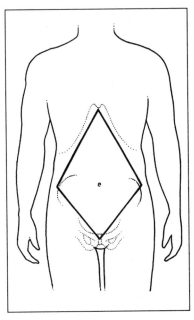

Janice Chapman has coined the term 'the diamond' for the supporting muscles of the abdominal wall on account of the shape formed by these four points.

1. In the previous two exercises we worked with the two sides of the waistband, the xyphoid process and the point just above the pubic arch. Put all four points together; you will need to alternate between them as you only have two hands!
2. Repeat the rolled 'R' or lip-blowing sequence moving up and down through your range.

Diagram 3: the diamond

Notice what happens. You should be working the four corners of the diamond while keeping the centre of the diamond flexible. It's simple and very effective.

Intra-abdominal pressure.

It may be difficult to visualise how work in the abdominal wall, which is admittedly a long way from the vocal folds, can help to maintain create sub-glottic pressure. Here is a very straightforward way of looking at this concept.

1. People often use a balloon as an image for the lungs. I want you to visualise two balloons: one representing the chest (upper) cavity, and one representing the abdominal (lower) cavity.

2. The abdominal cavity is sealed and separated from the chest cavity by the diaphragm. Because the diaphragm is flexible, it is possible to create pressure in the abdominal cavity and push the diaphragm upward into the chest cavity.

3. The chest cavity is not sealed. It has the valve of the vocal folds at the top end. The vibrating vocal folds can create 'back pressure' against the pressure sent up from the abdominal cavity, which in turn creates pressure in the chest. This back-pressure is the sub-glottic pressure that we need for singing.

We are doing something unnatural when we sing sustained passages of music; we are asking the body to let out the breath in a sustained manner while the pressure in the chest decreases. The body's normal response would be to breathe in as pressure in the chest drops. You will find, by creating this intra-abdominal pressure, that you are able to maintain pressure in the chest while you are doing sustained singing.

The muscles you are using when you work the 'diamond' to create intra-abdominal pressure are the external and internal oblique muscles and the transversus abdominis. All three muscles are paired (there is a set each side of the body), and are broad and flat in shape, attaching to the ribcage and parts of the pelvic crest. The transversus abdominis and internal obliques (the deeper layers) also link via tendons and connective tissue to the spinal column and so form a tube around the body.

These three sets of muscles, together with rectus abdominis at the front (the one we associate with the 'six-pack' effect), form a strong sheath for your abdominal contents. They are active in stabilising posture and in forward and sideways bends.

Exercise 3: WORKING TO SUSTAIN

1. Sing this five note scale to a rolled 'R' or to a lip-trill. Go up and down the scale in one breath.

2. Repeat the scale, this time starting a semitone (half-tone) higher.

Continue this sequence, allowing time to recoil in between each scale. Put in as many beats as you need at first to allow yourself time to recoil; you can always reduce the number and length of the beats in between as you become more experienced. There are no brownie points for doing the sequence without the recoil; it doesn't mean that you are developing your capacity to sustain if you do this, it means you are doing it wrong!

3. Extend the scale to this nine note scale given.

You'll find this takes a little more concentration on your waistband muscles. Surprisingly, you may find that you are not taking in any more air than you did for the five note scale; if this is the case, it is because you are beginning to use your breath more efficiently.

Some students are so fixated on breathing in that they never allow themselves to find the point when they run out of breath. I can remember one of my teachers congratulating me when I ran out of breath, and I have been known to do the same with my own students. In truth we hardly ever use up all our air because it is something the body does not like. You will start to feel 'out of breath' as you approach negative pressure in the lungs – a state where the air pressure is higher outside the body than in. Consequently you will feel as though you want to breathe in. In fact you don't have to at this point; you can override the response and keep working the abdominal wall until you really are at the end of your singing capacity. Remember to silently laugh in the larynx as you do this; you are more likely to constrict at negative pressure. Remember to recoil fully at the end of the last note in the phrase.

Posture

I mentioned earlier that the muscles of the abdominal wall are active in stabilising posture; you need them when you are standing or sitting up. I have not written about 'good' and 'bad' posture because I do not want to imply that posture is a fixed thing. The body is set up to work efficiently for many different tasks, and your posture will vary according to the task in hand.

In this instance if your standing posture is poor, the use of your abdominal wall will be poor too. If you do not have a good sense of where the support muscles are, you should go to an exercise class or to the gym and ask the instructor to devise a programme for you. People who are not toned often do not sing well. Exercises that put you in touch with these muscles – lateral bends, twists and curl-ups – will be helpful for your use of support. The Pilates system is very good for actors, and there are a number of classes available with trained instructors who understand the needs of the profession. For an efficient posture:

1. Stand with your feet comfortably apart (for most people this is at hip width) so that you have a solid base.

2. The knees should not be locked; locked knees put the whole spine out of balance and might cause you difficulties with the recoil breath.

3. Pay attention to the tilt of your pelvis; if you are over-arching your back and tipping the pelvis backwards, you will not get full movement from the diaphragm when you breathe in. Conversely do not slump the body by tipping the pelvis forwards; you cannot engage the muscles of the abdominal wall if you are slumped.

4. Keeping the head over the shoulders, feel that your spine is in alignment. Don't try to straighten the spine, but be aware of its full length.

5. The shoulders should be relaxed and the arms hanging easily.

6. Do not collapse the rectus abdominis along the front of the body, particularly just below the sternum. You may think you are relaxed when you are doing this, but you certainly won't be ready to sing! You will need to organise the front of your body so that you can utilise the top and bottom of your 'diamond' efficiently.

When I was training as a singer, it sometimes felt as though I was on a quest for the holy grail of 'the breath'! I realise now that there is no perfect breathing system, only a body of knowledge that performers and teachers have found to work in practice. Most of the work I do on breathing with my students is remedial: fixing bad habits and getting rid of inappropriate effort. On the whole I find that if a singer is not inhibiting the in-breath, and that all is well in the larynx, there is very little to be said about breathing. If you are having difficulties with your breathing, start by analysing the source of the problem. Ask yourself these questions:

1. Am I allowing myself to breathe in? (If not, work on the elastic recoil.)

2. Do I have sufficient airflow? (Test this with the rolled 'R' or lip trill.)

3. Am I over-breathing by taking in or pushing out too much air for the singing task? (Monitor your airflow and examine your onset of tone.) Some trained singers and actors are so obsessed with breathing that they do not let the vocal folds do their work of creating resistance to the breath, and then over-breathe.

If the information in this chapter is mostly new to you, I suggest you work through it in chunks. Don't try to understand it all at once. As you work through the rest of this book, it will be easy for you to forget the work we have done here. I will be reminding you to apply it as we go along. In particular, each time we work a new structure in the vocal instrument I will ask you to go through the Isolation Checklist from Chapter 2 (page 18). High up on that list is the instruction to release the abdominal wall or to *breathe in and out freely*; you should use the elastic recoil at this point and then move from active expiration to passive respiration (normal breathing), so that you isolate the breathing from whatever structure you are working at the time. Practise the exercises on a regular basis until you know what you should be feeling and where. As you build an awareness of airflow and resistance you will find that you have fewer breathing problems.

Section 2

How Do I Train?

How do you train a voice? If we are exercising our vocal muscles every day in the primary functions, and we did no 'training' in order to speak, do we need training to sing? The point is, although the mechanism is in place for singing, the programming is not. I believe this to be true even for those lucky people who seem to sing instinctively. Singing and speech are learned behaviour. Singing rhythms, pitches and words over an amplified band or an orchestra is most certainly learned behaviour! You need to train as a vocal athlete: gaining control over muscle groups and practising their use until you have maximum efficiency. The rest of your training is to do with style and artistry: an opera singer will train differently from a musical theatre singer and actor, who will train differently from a Bulgarian folk singer.

The focus of this book is on training appropriate to the modern actor, who may be called upon to sing in a range of vocal styles in dramatic productions. Modern musical theatre offers music in a broad range of styles, and the singing actor who hopes to stay in work must be prepared for this.

In this section we will be looking at developing range and controlling pitch. This will ensure that your vocal keyboard is in working order. You will learn control of the nasal port so that you can choose between nasal and oral resonance. Further work on resonance deals with the oral cavity and vowel placement, and the last chapter in this section deals with how to get brightness, or twang, into your sound. The other major issue covered is that of dynamic control: what is needed for loud and quiet singing, and how to work the body to make the vocal instrument bigger, and enable it to work harder.

You will be applying the techniques learned in Chapters 1–4:

Chapter 1: locating the soft palate; the siren;

Chapter 2: retraction; Isolation Checklist;

Chapter 3: raising, lowering, and tilting the larynx;

Chapter 4: airflow and elastic recoil; working the waistband.

You might also find it helpful to refer to the vowel and consonant keys on pages 45-7.

The purpose of the exercises that follow is to work specific muscle groups in order to gain strength (where this is applicable) and control. You'll notice that I do not give a lot of scales and arpeggios as exercises. It is my opinion that these are designed largely for instrumentalists who need to practise fingering routines. Unlike the majority of other instrumentalists we do not play our instrument with the fingers; the agility has to develop in the larynx, and we have to get in touch with it first. In my experience, if the voice production is wrong, scales and arpeggios – so-called vocalises – simply entrench bad habits. Once you have mastery of your instrument you can go on to apply the work in music and song. There are many instances in which you can exercise your voice through a song, rather than spending a lot of time 'preparing' your voice for singing. For this reason, many of the chapters will include a song assignment.

Warm-ups

Warm-ups are great if they are about being physically and mentally alert for the task in hand. You do not need to spend a lot of time warming up your voice in order to be able to practise. Just notice how long it takes you to be able to siren efficiently when starting the day and use this to programme your warm up time. If you know that you need to do something in the day before you start to work at your voice – maybe a stretching routine or going for a walk – that too should be part of your warm-up. Creating a mental space is also important; some actors will quietly read the paper as their preparation before going on stage. You will find out what is right for you. At this point in the book, your vocal warm-up should consist of: retraction, the siren, and a few minutes practice of the elastic recoil. All of these will prepare your vocal mechanism for the effort of singing. Once your siren is in place without any breaks, you are ready to go.

Standard British Vowel Key

Note: When the letter 'r' follows a vowel in the Interpretative spelling, it is not pronounced.

Phonetics	Interpretative spelling	Representative words
[ɑ:]	'AH'	task, rather, mark
[ɜ:]	'ER'	stern, bird, turf
[ɔ:]	'AW'	bored, walker, law
[i:]	'EE'	she, mean, feed
[u:]	'OO'	moves, crude, boots
[ɪ]	'ih'	kids, still, wished
[æ]	'ae'	sad, banned, splashed
[e]	'eh'	fresh, tenth, section
[ʌ]	'UH'	button, worried, wonders
[ɒ]	'aw'	what, soft, costly
[ʊ]	'ou'	look, pullets, put
[ə]	'uh'	the, alone, mother
[ɪə]	'ir'	near, fear, rear
[eə]	'air'	there, hair, fair
[ʊə]	'oor'	mature, poor, lure
[eɪ]	'ey'	they, say, away
[aɪ]	'ay'	time, high, awry
[ɔɪ]	'oy'	boy, loin, android
[əʊ]	'oh'	no, sew, ago
[aʊ]	'ow'	how, loud, vow
[eɪə]	'eyor'	player, conveyor, slayer
[aɪə]	'ire'	science, violet, fire
[ɔɪə]	'oyer'	lawyer, royal, toil
[əʊə]	'oer'	lower, mower, blower
[aʊə]	'ower'	power, sour, flower

Standard American Vowel Key

Note: 'rr' in an interpretative spelling means that the vowelised hard 'r' is present.

Phonetics	*Interpretative spelling*	*Representative words*
[ɑ:]	'AH'	f**a**ther, s**o**vereign, c**a**lm
[ɝ]	'URR'	p**er**fect, pref**er**, s**ur**geon
[ɒ:]	'aww'	th**aw**, wr**o**ng, s**aw**
[i:]	'EE'	sh**e**, m**ea**n, f**ee**d
[u:]	'OO'	m**o**ves, cr**u**de, b**oo**ts
[ɪ]	'ih'	k**i**ds, st**i**ll, w**i**shed
[æ]	'ae'	s**a**d, b**a**nned, spl**a**shed
[ɛ]	'eh'	fr**e**sh, t**e**nth, s**e**ction
[ʌ]	'UH'	w**a**s, wh**a**t, **u**nder
[ʊ]	'ou'	l**oo**k, p**u**llets, p**u**t
[ə]	'uh'	th**e**, **a**lone, tak**e**n
[ɚ]	'urr'	s**ur**prise, p**er**chance, moth**er**
[ɪɚ]	'irr'	r**ear**, n**ear**, app**ear**
[ɛɚ]	'err'	th**ere**, h**air**, f**air**
[ɑɚ]	'arr'	c**ar**, s**ar**dine, t**ar**
[ɔɚ]	'orr'	m**ore**, **Or**pheus, p**ore**
[ʊɚ]	'oorr'	p**ure**, end**ure**, cont**our**
[eɪ]	'ey'	th**ey**, s**ay**, aw**ay**
[aɪ]	'ay'	t**i**me, h**igh**, awr**y**
[ɔɪ]	'oy'	b**oy**, l**oi**n, andr**oi**d
[oʊ]	'oh'	**o**ver, ag**o**, v**o**gue
[aʊ]	'ow'	h**ow**, all**ow**, v**ow**
[eɪɚ]	'eyurr'	pl**ayer**, conv**eyor**, sl**ayer**
[aɪɚ]	'ayurr'	d**ire**, adm**ire**, f**ire**
[ɔɪɚ]	'oyurr'	l**awyer**, f**oyer**, empl**oyer**
[oʊɚ]	'ohurr'	l**ower**, m**ower**, bl**ower**
[aʊɚ]	'owurr'	p**ower**, s**our**, fl**ower**

Standard Consonant Key

Phonetics	Interpretative spelling	Representative words
[p]	'p'	**p**eel, a**pp**roach, stoo**p**
[b]	'b'	**b**ell, tri**b**ute, tu**b**e
[m]	'm'	**m**arry, ca**m**paign, handso**m**e
[f]	'f'	**f**ellow, a**f**ter, stu**ff**
[v]	'v'	**v**ery, a**v**erage, gi**v**e
[w]	'w'	**w**estern, stal**w**art, a**w**ay
[ʍ]	'hw'	**wh**at, **wh**ether, a**wh**ile
[θ]	'th'	**th**ink, a**th**lete, tru**th**
[ð]	'~~th~~'	**th**is, ra**th**er, bli**th**e
[t]	't'	**t**ime, fu**t**ile, ha**t**
[d]	'd'	**d**eep, a**dd**ition, be**d**
[s]	's'	**s**ip, a**ss**ume, bli**ss**
[z]	'z'	**z**est, pre**s**ume, head**s**
[l]	'l'	**l**ast, f**l**our, simi**l**ar
[ɫ]	'll'	pu**ll**, se**l**f, si**l**ver
[n]	'n'	**n**either, a**n**tique, fu**n**
[ʃ]	'sh'	**sh**ift, viciou**s**, po**sh**
[ʒ]	'ge'	bei**ge**, centrifu**ge**, rou**ge**
[tʃ]	'ch'	**ch**est, an**c**ient, lur**ch**
[dʒ]	'j'	**j**ump, a**dj**acent, ba**dge**
[ɹ]	'r'	**r**ed, a**rr**ow, **r**u**r**al
[j]	'y'	**y**esterday, can**y**on, vine**y**ard
[k]	'k'	**k**ept, sil**k**en, sha**ck**
[g]	'g'	**g**uest, be**g**otten, bi**g**
[ŋ]	'ng'	si**ng**, li**n**k, Li**n**coln
[ɲ]	'NY'	vi**gn**ette, **gn**occi, pi**ñ**a colada
[h]	'h'	**h**ave, a**h**ead, **h**uge
[ʔ]	' ' '	"'uh-'oh", "'eyyy!", "'ai!"

Chapter 5

Developing the three octave siren

The chapter title is not intended as a challenge; it's just that I've found most of my students have a three-octave range if their voices are healthy and they know how to work the muscles. There is no reason why you cannot achieve this. You can use the siren as the basis of your warm-up, to programme into your voice the notes of a song, to improve your sense of pitch, to work your whole range, and to eliminate breaks and cracks in the voice. Not bad for one exercise!

You are now starting to work with your voice. This means that you should practise the retraction or silent laugh posture described in Chapter 2 in order to release laryngeal constriction. You are not necessarily retracted in the larynx as a matter of course.

Exercise 1: LAUGHING AT THE LARYNX

1. Breathe out gently, shaping an 'EE' [i:] with the tongue but using no voice at all.
2. Continue to breathe out and constrict a little at the larynx. You will make a rasping sound now, somewhat like the constricted whispering of Marlon Brando in *The Godfather*. This happens because you are closing up the space above the vocal folds. Still let the sound come from the 'EE' [i:] shape in your mouth, the air and the constriction. You should not be voicing.
3. Now laugh silently at the larynx and notice what happens: immediately the constriction (and the rasping sound) disappears because you have opened up the space above the vocal folds.
4. Continue breathing out as you hold the retracted position. You may find that as soon as you have reached it, the air rushes out all at once. This is because there is nothing stopping it. You can attend to this by controlling the release of air from the abdominal wall, if you like, but it really doesn't matter at this stage. The important thing is to hold the laugh posture and to be able to breathe in or out.
5. Notice that holding the laugh posture requires effort. Don't lose that sense of effort; you are not relaxed when you are singing. As an aid to muscular memory, you may find it helpful to give the effort a 'number', with one being the least and ten being the most amount of effort you can make. What is your effort number in holding the laugh posture?

Make a mental note of it so that you can use it again.

Retraction, or maintaining the silent laugh posture, is fundamental to healthy singing. You should check yourself for it at the beginning of any practice session, during any part of rehearsing, or when you are learning or practising anything that you find difficult. I would also like you to check yourself for it as we go through the other exercise routines. The above exercise is the easiest way to check yourself; once you are laughing at the larynx you can continue with each new task.

In Chapter 1, Exercise 4, we did some sirening as an exercise in awareness. We looked at the sensations of effort that are associated with vocalising, and at the changes we can feel from inside the vocal mechanism as we move through our potential vocal range. Don't be surprised if it takes a matter of weeks for you to get your three octaves; it won't necessarily happen all at once.

Exercise 2: RANDOM SIRENING

1. Make sure that you are already retracted as you make a small whining sound on an 'ng' [ŋ] (as in the word 'sing'). For the 'ng', the back of your tongue is braced up against the soft palate and the tip of the tongue is resting behind the bottom front teeth. Just get used to this position, as it may feel closed at the back rather than open. If you are used to opening up at the back of the mouth in order to make sound, the siren can feel unusual.
2. Start to move the siren around a little, moving up and down in pitch like this:

   Notice that you need hardly any breath to make this sound and that, if you are in a comfortable part of your range, it takes very little effort. The sound should always be small and quiet as this is a 'feel' exercise. Note that you can stop and start the exercise at any point provided you are retracted when you start again. If you need to breathe, breathe – but my advice is to take in small amounts of air rather than a lot.
3. Make your siren go up and down further. Then go up and down as far as you can, noticing what you feel as you do so.
   Did you notice that:
   i. the larynx tends to move up and down with the pitch

ii. the tongue pushes up against the soft palate, more so as you go higher. You feel everything getting smaller at the back of the mouth as you go up in pitch;

iii. you can feel 'work' around the sides and back of the neck at different points in your range.

4. Do the whole sequence again, remembering to laugh at the larynx, to keep the sound quiet and small, to use only a little breath. Work through the Isolation Checklist (see page 18) at the same time:

i. chew with the front of your mouth as you siren at the back to get rid of jaw tension;

ii. check your alignment; lengthen the neck and elongate the whole spine;

iii. walk around the room so that you do not have unnecessary body tension.

You are now isolating specific muscle functions. In Chapter 2, we talked about the Isolation Checklist, and this is what I will refer to from now on.

If your voice cracks when you siren, it's OK; it just means you are normal. The voice, like any other pipe, is an imperfect instrument. You have changes of registration to deal with, meaning that your vocal folds must adjust their thickness, or mass, as you move through your range. As you go higher, the vocal folds need to become longer and thinner. The reverse will happen as you go lower: the vocal folds must bulk up and become shorter and thicker. Until you become used to managing these changes of gear or registration, your voice may crack or break. Also the larynx needs to rise for high notes; this is the same movement as in swallowing and might trigger constriction. Any changes or extra work in the larynx can trigger constriction if you do not maintain the silent laugh posture; this is why your voice may cut out until you can learn to manage these changes. Here's how to deal with this problem.

Exercise 3: TARGETING YOUR BREAKS

1. Go up (or down) to the point where your siren has a break point or cuts out on you. Notice if your habit is to constrict at this difficult point in your range, and use the silent laugh.

2. Next time, as you approach the same place, slow down before you get there and pay attention. Put your hand to the back of your neck, at the base of the skull where there is a slight depression (the occipital groove). Push up and back with the base of your skull into your hand. This will have the effect of straightening the cervical spine and giving support to the larynx as you change gear. You need to maintain this posture for a few notes only and then should be able to continue with no trouble.

3. Work through all the change points in your range in this way until you can make a smooth transition from the bottom to the top of your range. It is not unusual to have two significant change points to negotiate.

This is rather like learning to drive a car with gearshifts: as you increase speed, you move up a gear. In order to change gear, you have to engage the clutch. The lengthening of the cervical spine is like dipping the clutch. As with a good driver, we should not hear the change though you will always feel it. Practise ironing out your changes of registration by working in a figure of eight in pitch round and around the problem notes. With practice, you will get your three octave siren!

Problems with sirening

Sometimes, if the tongue is too low, a student will have difficulty reaching the top of the siren. Remind yourself that the high notes are made with a smaller space, not bigger. The vocal folds are working harder when you sing a high note (look again at the frequencies I quoted on page 5) so you will need a harder silent laugh. The larynx rises for high notes, making the space smaller, which may be opposite to your image of high notes. If you are having trouble reaching the higher notes, check that you are sirening with 'EEng' [iːŋ] and not 'UHng' [ʌŋ], and try sirening with the sides of the tongue touching the upper back molars to keep the tongue high. Do not push down with the tongue as you go up in pitch.

If your siren is breathy and raspy, you are almost certainly making the mistake of pushing air. You need hardly any breath for a siren; if you push air through the siren (driving breath), you will force the vocal folds apart and the tone will be breathy. To combat this, do Exercise 1 (page 48) to retract the false vocal folds, and breathe out most of your air. Then, siren on what is left. The breathiness will clear, and you will make a cleaner sound. Using this as a starting point, you will be able to work out for yourself how much breath you need for the full siren.

Practising pitch and agility

So far you have been working the siren as a noise. Doing it to specific pitches is just the same. I always siren in octave leaps as it's a good way to practise pitch and agility. The extent of your siren will depend on the boundaries of your range; no voice is the same as another. If you are unsure about your range, work through the following exercise with a vocal coach or friend who plays keyboard, and 'chart' your range, including the change points. You may be surprised to find that your range now encompasses two-and-a-half to three octaves; this is quite easy to achieve if you work the siren correctly. If you don't read music it doesn't matter; working the siren will improve your feel for pitch so that you will begin to know where you are in your voice even without accompaniment.

Exercise 4: OCTAVE SIRENS

1. Using the same amount of effort as before, siren up an octave from a low note and back again.

2. Keep the silent laugh posture after you've finished the leap and take a small breath in.
3. Move up a step and repeat.

4. Continue on up, step by step until you reach the top of your range.
5. Keeping the octave leap, work your way down again, step by step.
   I often find that the siren goes haywire when the student starts to sing it. Remember that it is exactly the same process as before and:
   i. don't push air;
   ii. keep your tongue and palate together at all times, even for the high notes;
   iii. siren softly, gliding between pairs of notes so that there are no gaps (essentially you are singing all the pitches in-between the two notes, but very fast);
   iv. notice where you feel your soft palate wanting to lift and the larynx rising; at this point push up with your tongue and palate together;
   v. push back with the base of the skull and lengthen the cervical spine as you negotiate any change points.

Moving from sirening to vowels

All the time you were doing the octave sirens in Exercise 4, your tongue and palate were together and the sound was, in fact, coming down your nose. Now you are going to take the sound into vowels. I always start with 'EE' [i:] as it is the easiest to sing. Look at the musical example opposite which illustrates stages 1 and 2 for Exercise 5:

ng – EE_____

You'll see that in stage two you are going to change from 'ng' [ŋː] to 'EE' once you have hit the top note. This requires you to move your soft palate away from the back of the tongue. If you are unsure about this, look back at Chapter 1, page 10, where I have explained how to locate the soft palate. There are further exercises for the palate in Chapter 6 as well.

Exercise 5: FROM SIREN TO VOWEL

This is a variation of Exercise 4.

1. Using the same notes as before, glide up the octave on 'ng' and sing the top note a little longer as you move from 'ng' to 'EE'.
2. Come down again still singing 'EE' and keeping everything else the same as for the siren: the silent laugh, the neck lengthening, the amount of breath and so on. The only thing you have changed is the position of the soft palate. The sound will still be quiet, but it should be clear and sound 'easy'.
3. You can do this with other vowels as well, but always start with 'EE'.

This exercise with the octave glides is almost the only one I do as it has many variations. It requires no accompaniment and can be done anywhere. It will not disturb the neighbours and it will warm and 'tune up' your voice very efficiently! We will return to it later. You can also use the same principle with the notes of a song by sirening the melody. (See the song assignment at the end of this chapter.)

Trouble with pitching

A lot of nonsense is fed to singers who have difficulties with pitching, and this includes the much over-used term 'tone-deaf'. I don't hold with the term tone-deaf: 99% of people who can't sing in tune can hear melodies; they just have difficulty in reproducing them. Over and again I have found that dealing with laryngeal constriction – enabling the vocal folds to vibrate properly – goes a long way towards solving pitch problems. It is interesting that when someone has a difficulty with pitch, we try to teach him or her to sing in tune by either singing scales or bashing out single notes on the piano (the 'can't you hear that?' technique). People with pitching problems do not know how to make the link between what they are feeling in the vocal tract, and what they are hearing. Pitch needs to be felt as well as heard.

Exercise 6: FEELING THE PITCH

1. Start by getting 'in touch' with the vocal mechanism so that you can rely on kinaesthetic feedback, not just auditory. Work with retraction and simply sing your own notes.

2. Next work the siren: it helps you to map out the feeling of up and down. It also builds into your muscle memory how hard you are working in certain parts of your range.

3. Siren without trying to make notes at all at first; just make the noise. Then work with big intervals. (Note that it is not desirable for novice singers to start with the fine-tuning. We do not ask children when they are learning to write to begin with calligraphy; we allow them to make big movements!)

4. Avoid working with the piano! The piano is tuned according to what is known as equal temperament, which makes it difficult for the human ear to differentiate easily between one interval and another. When you are learning to pitch, get your teacher or vocal coach to sing the notes for you preferably at pitch in your octave.

5. Work the siren on vowels as well as 'ng' [ŋ:], working from the octave to intervals of a 5th to a 3rd and so on. Gradually you will begin to trust the connection between your voice and your ear.

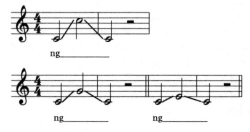

6. Work with Exercises 1, 2, 3, and 5 in Chapter 6 for the soft palate and control of the nasal port. You will begin to feel you can organise the different sensations you have in your instrument, and will build in reliable muscular feedback. The soft palate exercises are very physical and will give you something to 'pin the notes on'.

7. Move on to the anchoring: Exercises 1-5 in Chapter 7. Many people are singing the right pitch but sound out of tune because the note isn't resonating properly. I have found this particularly with singers who have big voices. A big voice in the early stages of training will often be somewhat wild in its pitching. Using an analogy, how would you do in your first driving lesson if someone put you behind the wheel of a Porsche or a Daimler? Anchoring will help you to resonate better and give you control over the size of your voice.

So that's it. Now you have the full keyboard for your instrument. Whether or not it is three octaves, remember that if you can siren it, you can sing it!

Song assignment: YOUR SONG

Find a song; almost any song will do. Choose one that you do not know very well yet, but for which you have either the sheet music or a reliable recording.

1. Listen to the melody or play it on a keyboard.
2. Phrase by phrase, or with any small unit of the melodic line, siren your way through the song. Make sure that you siren seamlessly between pitches that belong together in the same phrase. Inexperienced singers will often try to hit each note with the vocal folds in order to check their tuning. Remember that the voice is not a percussion instrument. If two notes belong together in one phrase, and there is no rest, there is no need for the vocal folds to stop vibrating before pitching the next note. The pitching mechanism is in the larynx: if you are set up correctly, your vocal folds will soon make the minute adjustments required to change pitch without much prompting from you.
3. Breathe with the sense of the words wherever possible, and put in the rests where they are written (or indicated on the recording). When you are learning a new song, it doesn't matter how many times you need to breathe; just do what is comfortable to begin with. As your muscles begin to learn the shape of the melody, you will find that the breathing becomes easier.
4. Check that you are retracted all the time. A good way to do this is to sing the song silently, mouthing the words as you go, and breathing out as if you were singing. This way you can concentrate on maintaining the laugh posture and listen with the muscles. It also gives you the opportunity to observe what is going on in the abdominal wall – are you allowing the abdominal wall to release as you recoil into each new breath?
5. Siren the song again.
6. Repeat the song with the words; you are already programming the song into your muscular memory. This is part of a process that we shall use later in the book when we look at how to learn new material quickly.
7. Make a note of any corners that you find difficult in the song. Are you constricting on these notes? Are they at change points in your range? You can solve these problems with the techniques you have learned in this chapter.

Chapter 6

Controlling the nasal port

Many clients come to me for a voice assessment or trouble-shooting session. Often they are working professionals who have got into singing in the course of their career and simply have not had the time to sort out what they are doing technically. Surprisingly often in the course of an assessment I will ask, 'Do you know you are leaking air through the nose and that your tone is nasal?' We will then have a discussion about the nose, the mouth and the nasal port. Many people have no concept of the nasal port, and among those that do there is often confusion. Here are a few common misconceptions:

1. The soft palate is always up when you are singing.
2. The soft palate lifts automatically when you breathe in.
3. You have no independent control over the soft palate.
4. You will get a brighter tone if you sing into your nose.
5. The contemporary musical theatre sound is nasal.

THE NASAL PORT

Look at Diagram 1: the sagittal section of the vocal tract.

If you look at the hard palate, which forms the roof of the mouth, you will see that it extends into a non-bony area (the shaded areas indicate bone in the diagram) and ends in the uvula. You can feel this if you run your tongue backwards along the roof of the mouth until you reach the soft, fleshy area and the dangling uvula. Now look at Diagrams 2-4, which show how the palate can move. Notice that it can either:

1. seal itself against the back of the tongue, stopping any sound from going out of the mouth (Diagram 2), or,

2. make a seal with the back of the pharynx, stopping any sound from going into the nose (Diagram 4).

This 'sealing' action is why we talk about the nasal port: it is a doorway between the mouth and the nose. *When your nasal port is open the palate is down* and the sound will be nasal; *when your nasal port is closed the palate is up* and the sound will be oral. You can also have a half-open nasal port (Diagram 3); this is when the soft palate is relaxed and sound is coming through both the nose and mouth.

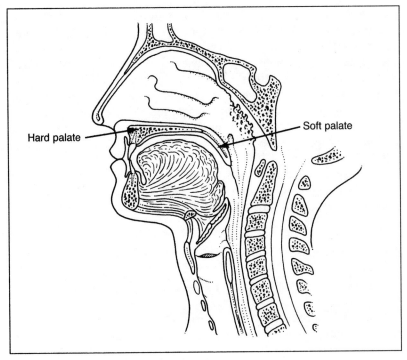

Diagram 1: the sagittal section of the vocal tract

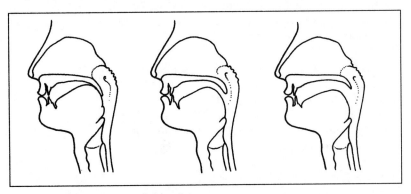

Diagrams 2-4: positions of the palate

Gaining control over the nasal port is an essential part of adjusting your resonance and correct vowel formation. You will also find that working the palate muscle will help you in preparation of top notes.

The muscles responsible for making the seal are the levator and tensor palatinis. A combined effort between these two muscles and your soft palate make the seal between the nose and mouth. The palatinis will raise and tense the palate so that it can pull up and back towards the pharyngeal wall. Another muscle that you can feel working if you do this with effort is the palato pharyngeus, which acts as a support in the sealing action by firming up the wall of the pharynx. All this is happening deep inside the skull. When you work the palate exercises that follow, you will feel effort in an imaginary line from the base of the skull to your hard palate. For this reason, you can see how important it is not to collapse the cervical spine if you want your palate to work efficiently. People with poor head and neck posture often have difficulty with soft palate control.

You may be wondering how you can feel all this. Actually we don't have many sensory nerve endings in the soft palate so it isn't easy to isolate, but you can feel the effects of its movement very easily. Here is an exercise in awareness:

Awareness exercise I: FEELING THE SEAL BETWEEN THE ORAL AND NASAL CAVITIES

1. Make a firm 'ng' [ŋ] sound, but somewhat more forcefully than when you do the siren.
2. Now hold your nose but try to keep on singing.
3. Keep holding the nose and turn your 'ng' into a 'gEE' [giː].

Did you feel what happened? The 'ng' stopped when you held your nose because all the sound was coming down there. You could also feel that the air was being stopped. However, when you sang 'gEE', the air and sound was released into the mouth.

Here are some practice routines for the soft palate.

Exercise I: OPENING THE NASAL PORT

Sing 'hEEng' [hiːŋ], making the air come through the nose as you say the 'h'. Put a lot of effort into the 'h'. Your palate should come down sharply onto the back of the tongue.

Exercise 2: CLOSING THE NASAL PORT

1. Start with the 'ng' [ŋ] and then make a 'g' [g] very strongly as you say 'ng-gEE' [ŋgiː]. The consonant 'g' is a voiced stop made with the soft palate. As you make the 'g', your palate is first held against the tongue, then released, so you should feel it quite strongly.
2. Do this again, making the 'g' as big as you can. Still do the 'ng' first so that the nasal port is opened, then closed.

Exercise 3: OPENING AND CLOSING THE NASAL PORT

1. Practise opening and closing on one note: 'h-ng-gEE'–'h-ng-gEE' [hŋgiː–hŋgiː], making the lift-off from the final 'g' as big as you can each time.
2. Repeat this with other vowels from the vowel key on pages 45-6. Make sure that you can close your port equally well on all the vowels.

Exercise 4: HALF-OPEN TO CLOSED

It is helpful to use external monitoring for this exercise: place your fingers just underneath the nostrils so that you can feel for changes in airflow.

1. Make a conscious effort to sing down your nose as you say 'hEE'-'hEH'-'hAH'-'hAW'-'hOO' [hiː]-[he]-[hɑː]-[hɔː]-[huː]. It helps if you don't open the jaw much and try to direct the airflow through the nose. The sound will be quite muffled. You should feel the vibrations against your fingers as you touch the holes of the nostrils. (Sometimes a handkerchief is needed during this exercise!)
2. Now feel the difference as you go from half-open to closed. Start with a nasalised 'EE' [ĩː] (˜ is the symbol for nasalised sounds). Then close the nasal port by raising the soft palate; the sound will be louder and clearer.

   This is the point where many students feel confused as it is very difficult to feel whether the palate is up or down, let alone halfway anything! Use external monitoring again:
3. Pinch your nostrils firmly as you sing the nasalised 'EE'. Your fingers will tell you that you are blocking off some of the air and the sound.
4. Keep singing the nasalised 'EE', but try to stop the air from coming down your nose. The sensation of relief as you close the port will be similar to what you do to make your ears pop on an aeroplane when there is a sudden change in pressure. There should now be no air coming down your nose as you sing the 'EE' [iː].

If you cannot close your nasal port efficiently when you are singing, you will lose a considerable amount of resonance. The oral cavity is a more efficient resonator than the nasal cavity as it is bigger, and has less soft tissue and other substances that will dampen the sound. With oral resonance the sound will be brighter as well as louder. So acoustically it makes sense to sing with the nasal port closed.

Note that:

    1. You cannot form the vowels properly if the port is open. There are only three sounds in Standard English that are done with the nasal port open: 'n' [n], 'm' [m] and 'ng' [ŋ]. *Everything else should be done with the nasal port closed.*

In Standard American speech there is a higher degree of nasality than in Standard British, particularly on the vowels 'AH' [ɑː] and 'AW' [ɔː]. This is largely due to the higher tongue placement in American speech: there are muscles linking the tongue and plate that may depress the palate if the palatal raisers are not working hard enough (see Exercise 6). In singing American, you should form the vowels with the nasal port closed as this produces a more vibrant tone.

2. You are likely to have problems with airflow if you sing with your nasal port open all the time. The breath has further to travel up to the nasal cavity and the flow is being directed into two places, so you will run out of breath more quickly.

3. The soft palate contracts and is lifted up as you prepare for high notes in singing. The exercises will help you to do this when you need it.

These are the circumstances under which the nasal port will be open in singing:

1. It needs to be totally open for 'n', 'm' and 'ng'. Every time you sing a word containing one of these consonants – such as 'and' – your nasal port will be opening and closing as you sing it. See Song Assignment 3 at the end of this chapter for practice in singing syllables with nasal consonants.

2. Humming exercises on 'm'.

3. You can use the opening of the nasal port to make a very effective decrescendo. It's very effective in chorus when you have to sing very softly. (See Exercise 7 on page 63.)

There is nothing wrong with nasality as a vocal quality provided it is a conscious choice. Nasality is used a lot in commercial singing and works very well if the singer has amplification.

I am often asked if nasality is part of the West End or Broadway sound. I don't think it is. I think what we hear in good West End singing is 'twang'. I hear a lot of people who are trying to get what they think of as the West End sound by being nasal, but I think it is a misunderstanding that leads to inefficient vocalising. There is a nasalised version of twang which you can use safely and it would be appropriate in a pop-based musical. Overall there seems to be a lot of confusion over nasality and twang. Twang is a voice quality that has a particular resonance and it is made in the larynx. We will look at twang in Chapter 9, and I will tell you more about these differences then. For the time being, all you have to do is perform one simple test to see of your nasal port is open or closed: simply hold your nose. If you are singing vowels and the sound doesn't change, your port is closed and your sound is not nasal.

The next two exercises can be sung with accompaniment if you can get it.

Exercise 5: OPENING AND CLOSING THE NASAL PORT WHILE SINGING SCALES

1. On a descending scale sing 'ng-gEE' [ŋgiː] thus:

ng-gEE ng-gEE ng-gEE ng-gEE   ng-gEE ng-gEE ng-gEE ng-gEE

You will be opening and closing the nasal port on each note.
Be aware of the following:
i. The work is done at the back of the mouth, so keep your jaw relaxed. You might want to look in a mirror to check you are not 'mouthing' with the jaw.
ii. The back of the tongue needs to be high to meet the palate; the tip of the tongue should be out of the way behind the bottom front teeth.
iii. The action of the palate on the tongue should be energetic; make a hard 'g' as you do the 'lift off' each time into the vowel. Aim to do this by moving the palate, not dropping the tongue.
iv. Watch out for constriction. We close the port as a preparation for swallowing, so remember to retract!
v. If you are used to 'making space' for high notes, you will want to stop doing the 'ng' as you ascend in pitch. Do not allow this to happen: keep your palate and tongue 'glued together' when you make the 'ng'.
vi. Notice if you are lazy with your palate as you go to the bottom of your range. A lot of people lower the palate as they think 'down'; keep the work in the 'g' equally hard at all times.
Do this sequence as slowly as you need to to begin with, taking small top-up breaths at any point. Most people need a lot of thinking time for this exercise; you can increase the speed later.
Over and again, I have found that teaching this exercise, in addition to control of the nasal port, enables easy access to the top of the range.
2. Repeat the sequence on all the vowels in turn ('ng-gAH' 'ng-gAW', 'ng-gOO', etc), or on any combination of vowels.
Watch out for the following:
i. Make sure you can close your port equally well on all the vowels. Even with the back vowels where the back of the tongue is high – 'OO' [uː] for example – you can still get a closed port.
ii. Remember to round the lips on 'AW' [ɔː], 'aw' [ɒ], and 'OO' [uː].
Once you have mastered these exercises and can increase your speed, move onto the next stage, which should be done at speed.
3. Ascend the scale, going through a full octave singing through five vowels at a time and taking a breath whenever you need it.

ng-gAH ng-gEH ng-gEE ng-gAW ng-gOO   ng-gAH ng-gEH ng-gEE *etc*

This is a wonderful exercise for co-ordinating the action of the muscles in the oral cavity: soft palate, lips and tongue. As before, leave the jaw out of the act!

The palato pharyngeus muscle can help you to make a really good seal between the nose and the mouth. If you look at Diagram 5 showing the front view of the inside of the mouth, you will see that the palato pharyngeus is deep to the soft palate itself.

The next exercise forms a link with the following chapter on dynamic control, as it introduces the notion of anchoring the tone.

Exercise 6: WORKING THE PALATO PHARYNGEUS

In this exercise, you are looking for a sensation of effort deep to the soft palate. It will feel like something happening behind the nose and into the back of the neck.

1. At a slow speed, open and close the nasal port by singing: 'hng-gEE' [hŋgiː]. Pinch your nose when you reach the vowel.
2. Still singing 'EE' [iː], keep hold of the nose and try to 'pull' harder where you felt the port close; notice that the sound becomes fuller and more resonant. Make a note of where you feel the effort and how hard you are working.
3. Now take your fingers away from the nose.
4. Repeat the sequence, gliding into other vowels from the 'EE': 'hng-gEE-eh-AH-AW-OO' [hŋgiːeɑːɔːuː].
   Watchpoints:
   i. Monitor constriction; silently laugh at the larynx.
   ii. Keep the jaw out of the act; if it is tense, do a little chewing while you are singing.
   iii. Do not tense your tongue; roll it around inside the mouth if it is tensing unnecessarily.
   iv. Do not try to sing louder; the increase in sound does not happen in the vocal folds. It is probably a result of making a resonator out of your vocal tract.
5. Practise the sequence again without the nose-holding.

Years ago, I used to teach a version of this exercise at a drama college. When I demonstrated it, the students would sometimes accuse me of 'cheating', saying I was singing a different note! They heard the two sounds as different pitches because there was such a big change in resonance: the brightness harmonics were enhanced by the work in the soft palate and palato pharyngeus.

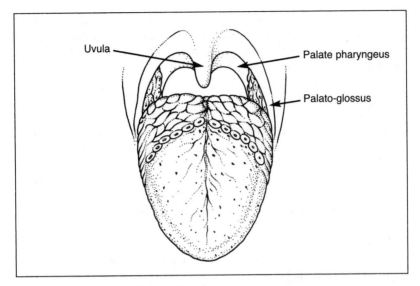

Diagram 5: front view of the oral cavity

Exercise 7: CONTROLLING A DECRESCENDO WITH THE SOFT PALATE

By opening your nasal port on a long note, you can make an effective decrescendo.

1. Sing the vowel 'EE' [iː], checking that your nasal port is closed by pinching the nostrils as you sing.
2. Keeping everything else exactly the same, gradually lower your soft palate towards the tongue as if going to make an 'ng' [ŋ].
3. Stop before you get to the 'ng' and hold this position. This is actually quite difficult to do and you may find that, at first, you cannot stop halfway. Just practise! When you are successful, you will be producing a nasalised 'EE' [ĩː].

4. Now do the same manoeuvre slowly singing the word 'end'. Sing the vowel for as long as you can, making a gradual transition to the nasal 'n' before the final 'd'.

If you are doing a lot of ensemble work and cannot sing softly enough for your musical director, use this technique of half-open port singing for the long notes. (In Chapter 7, you will learn to thin your vocal folds to make the sound less at the larynx too.)

Mirening

Mirening – a word coined by a student on an Estill course – comes from mouthing and sirening. To miren means to sing the notes on the 'ng' [ŋ] siren while mouthing the words at the front of the mouth. When you do this, you'll find that you can still shape most of the consonants (though not the ones that require you to use the palate, such as 'k' and 'g'). You can also shape the body of the tongue and the lips for the different vowels.

Exercise 8: MIRENING

1. Look at the words and melody from the beginning of *'The way you look tonight'* by Jerome Kern.

2. Put an 'ng' [ŋ] at the beginning of each syllable. If a word begins with a consonant, e.g. 'some', or 'day', you will sing 'ng-ome' [ŋʌm], or 'ng-ay' [ŋeɪ], while still forming the 's' or 'd' with the tongue tip.
3. Make sure you form all the vowel sounds correctly as you sing the words, still making the siren at the back of the mouth.
   Mirening requires considerable co-ordination. It is a great way to programme into your muscle memory the notes and words of a song.

Song assignment 1: YOUR SONG

1. Work with the song that you chose for the Song Assignment at the end of Chapter 5. Record yourself doing the following routines:
   i. singing the song once through;

ii. mirening the song; remember to keep the 'ng' at the back of the mouth all the way through this part of the exercise;

iii. singing the song with a half-open nasal port.

You will probably find that the half-open port singing takes a lot of breath. This doesn't matter. Just do the exercise and notice what you feel.

2. Listen back to the recording. You will probably notice that the half-open port affected your tuning as well as your breath use. There is less resonance when the port is open and it can make your tuning flat. You'll also notice that the vowels have less 'presence'.

Song assignment 2: HAPPY BIRTHDAY

'*Happy Birthday*' has no nasal consonants in it provided you sing the third line as 'happy birthday, happy birthday'. It's also a song that covers a range of one octave and so can be used as an exercise, going up or down in key.

1. Test your ability to close the nasal port by singing the whole song with your fingers just touching underneath the nostrils. If the port is closed, you should feel no air coming down the nose.

2. Practise the song in different keys, i.e. from different starting notes in your range.

Song assignment 3: AMAZING GRACE

A song without nasal consonants is pretty rare, so you need to know what happens when you sing these sounds. Let's look at the first phrase of '*Amazing Grace*', which we shall be working later on in the book:

The nasal consonants are underlined. Each time you sing one of these, the nasal port must open; when you go into the vowel that follows, the port must close up again.

1. Sing this phrase slowly, making sure that the sound really is coming down the nose for the sounds 'm', 'ng' and 'n'. Do the nose test to check.

A - m - az - ing ___ Grace, how sweet the sound

2. As you approach each of these nasal consonants and as you come out of them, check that the nasal port is closed.

It is not uncommon to start opening the port early when a nasal consonant is coming up at, say, the end of a word. This is not wrong, it's a matter of taste. For now, to demonstrate that you have control over this structure, keep the port closed until you actually get to the nasal consonant.

3. Each time you learn a new song, make a note of the nasal consonants and be aware of what is happening with your soft palate.

Understanding and controlling the nasal port is fundamental to building a sound vocal technique. Many people need to work hard at controlling the nasal port. This is largely because of habitual speech patterns: all along the Thames Estuary there are regional characterised by a degree of nasality, as well as in much of the Midlands and in Liverpool. There is nothing wrong with regional accents, of course, but sometimes you have to change the muscles patterning that comes with them in order to sing better. The same goes for singing in Standard US. You don't want nasality to creep into your sung vowels unless you have made a specific choice to include it. The great thing about the nasal port exercises is that you choose whatever is appropriate for you, for the style of music, and for the space you are singing in.

Chapter 7

Dynamic control and projection

So far, you have learnt how to siren through your entire range, how to eliminate cracks and breaks in your voice, and how to gain control over your nasal port. Now you need to learn about projection. How do you fill the space in a theatre? Don't kid yourself that it's all down to amplification nowadays; the band is miked as well. You will need to project, and that's why nearly all West End auditions are done in the working space and without amplification. (Some of the pop shows such as *Buddy* will audition with standing mikes because they are part of the act.) Singing in a large theatre space can be quite daunting and one of the things you will have to rely upon is the work done in the body to support your sound, otherwise you will push and drive the voice.

Several years ago a student of mine who was completing his final year at college was called to audition for Andrew Lloyd Webber's *Sunset Boulevard* at the Adelphi Theatre. Out of the entire year, he had always had the biggest voice, being a very able singer and having a lot of twang. This was his first professional audition and, although it went well, he was astonished to find – probably for the first time in his life – that he could not hear any sound coming back at him! 'It was really weird; I didn't know if they could hear me!' he said. We discussed going for kinaesthetic rather than auditory feedback for the recall and he was much happier the next time. The exercise routines in this chapter will help you to develop your own feedback for how hard you are working when you are singing at different dynamic levels: in the larynx, in other structures in the vocal tract, and in the body.

PROJECTION, OR HIGH INTENSITY VOCALISATION

Let's look first at the concept of projection. For high intensity vocalisation three conditions are required:

1. A deeper breath is needed;
2. The vocal folds must be closed for longer for each portion of the vibratory cycle;
3. Greater sub-glottic pressure is needed to create intense pressure ways for the ear of the listener.

This means is that there is a change in the vocal folds when we sing louder; it is not just about breath. In Chapter 4, I discussed the combined effect of airflow and vocal fold resistance – known as sub-glottic pressure. The resistance in the vocal folds is greater when you are singing louder. When you are singing louder you will also need to work the body; this will give support to the extra work in the vocal folds. You should also monitor your airflow in loud singing so that you do not push the vocal folds.

There is a way of making your sound appear louder (to the listener) without increased effort in the vocal folds, which involves twang. (We shall look at twang in Chapter 9.) First, let's consider how we monitor effort when we sing.

Awareness exercise 1: MONITORING EFFORT IN THE VOCAL FOLDS

When you are sirening, you are only making a tiny amount of effort in the vocal folds.

1. Prepare for the siren by silently mewing or whining. Remember to silently laugh at the larynx.
2. Keeping the same feeling in the larynx, sing very gently and quietly on 'ng-EE-eh-AH-AW-OO' [ŋiːeaːɔːuː], gliding from the 'ng' onto the vowels. You will probably be able to do this several times before you run out of breath; when you are singing softly the airflow is low.
3. Notice what is happening in your abdominal wall and your back as you go through the exercise for the 3rd or 4th time: muscles are working down there to hold the breath back!
   The thyroid cartilage is tilted for this quiet singing so it will help if you pull up and back in the cervical spine (see Chapter 5).
4. Now compare that with the following:
   i. Revise the glottal onset (Awareness exercise 2, Chapter 2) by saying 'uh-oh'.
   ii. Say 'EE' [iː], using the same attack as for the glottal onset.
   iii. Pitching close to your speaking voice sing the 'EE', keeping the same feeling.
   iv. Repeat this and continue the tone going through the vowels.
   Remember that at all stages you should have been retracted.

Did you feel your vocal folds working harder in the second part of the exercise? The vocal folds were thicker and stayed closed for longer. The resulting sound should have been louder. In order to be safe when singing loud, you will need to bring other muscles into play too; people who use just their vocal folds to get louder are driving the voice and will end up with problems.

Awareness exercise 2: RESISTING THE BREATH

Sometimes if you are very relaxed in the muscles when singing, the vocal folds will be vibrating but not actually closing.

1. Sing or speak a note with an aspirate onset, or 'h', as in singing on the breath. (We did this in Awareness exercise 3, Chapter 2.)
2. Putting your hand up close to your mouth, feel the air on your hand before the tone starts: 'hEE' [hiː].
3. Work through this vowel sequence, which starts with the back vowels: 'hOO HAW hAH heh hEE'[huː hɔː haː he hiː].

If you were relaxed in doing this, the resulting tone would have been breathy. In the larynx you were not working very hard and the body was relaxed too. Nearly all of your effort would have been in sending the breath up through your vocal folds. When you sing like this, the vocal fold muscles are offering very little resistance to the breath. There is nothing wrong with this; in fact the sound can be quite attractive, but it doesn't project very well without amplification and can be tiring if you do it all the time.

Postural anchoring

I've already mentioned that you need to increase the work in the vocal tract and in the body to get more volume. This is one aspect of 'support' as discussed in Chapter 4. Techniques for anchoring the tone have been described over the centuries by singers and teachers under a variety of names: support, singing from the back, singing from the neck, appoggiare (Italian for 'to lean'), rooting, grounding and connecting the voice. In the Estill training model, I believe these techniques have been correctly identified as postural anchoring. By anchoring the body we make a firm scaffolding for the vibrating mechanism of the voice and a solid resonating case for our instrument. It's also possible that anchoring improves our breath use, giving a boost to the muscles used in expiration; at least, this is a common perception.

There are rules to remember about anchoring:

1. The greater the vocal task, the harder you must work to support the vibrating mechanism.
2. Isolation is essential to anchoring.

Here's the Isolation Checklist that we used in Chapters 2 and 5.

1. Laugh silently to retract the false vocal folds.
2. Release the abdominal wall so that you can breath in and out easily – check this by saying the voiced fricatives 'v' and 'z' while you are anchored and recoil with the breath between each sound. You can then breathe normally.

3. Relax the mouth, jaw and the tongue by chewing and rolling the tongue around inside the mouth.
4. Move around the room, walking briskly.
5. Siren quietly or make small sounds on vowels to check you are not transferring too much work into the vocal folds.

Whenever you are doing the exercises for anchoring, you should go through the Isolation Checklist.

Anchoring the vocal tract.

You can feel the vocal tract being anchored from outside at the cervical spine, around the sides of the neck, across the front of the face, from inside at the soft palate and deep to it, and inside the mouth.

You already know where the cervical spine is and how to actively straighten it to give support to the larynx (see Exercise 3, Chapter 5). You can also feel the vocal tract widening at the front where the sternocleidomastoid muscles are (SCMs for short). Look at Diagram 1 opposite. To locate the SCMs turn your head to the left and feel for the muscle at the side of your neck on the right as it contracts. Follow the course of that muscle and you will feel that it goes down onto the dip of your collarbone and up behind the ear to the mastoid process. If you turn your head to the right, you'll locate the partner muscle on the other side.

Exercise 1: ANCHORING WITH THE CERVICAL SPINE AND SCMs

1. First try to straighten the cervical spine by lengthening and pulling slightly back. You can monitor this from outside by putting a couple of fingers into the base of the skull at the occipital groove and feeling for the adjustment you make. Take your hand away and keep the anchored position for the neck.
2. Now feel for the SCMs. Put one hand around the sides of the neck near the front, and make the other hand into a fist which you put against the forehead.
3. Keeping the back of the neck lengthened, press the fist against the forehead and push back against the fist with the forehead. This is a very effective way to get the SCMs working. Push until you can feel the SCMs beginning to work.

Watch out for the following:

i. You should be able to breathe in and out gently and freely at all stages during this exercise;

ii. Try to keep the work isolated in the head and neck area only; you do not need to involve the shoulders and you do not need to clamp the jaw;

iii. When you lengthen one part of your spine, something must happen in the rest of it. You could try the exercise seated to begin with, making sure that your back is in alignment. When you come to practise this

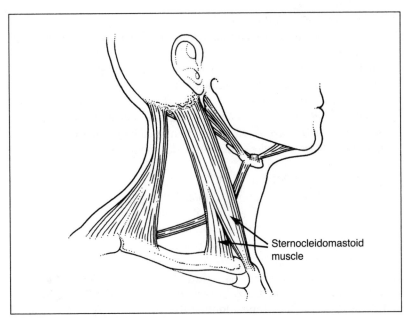

Diagram 1: the sternocleidomastoid muscles (SCMs)

exercise standing up, do not lock the knees. The base of the spine should be slightly tucked under.

4. Repeat the whole exercise, really paying attention this time to monitoring effort.
5. Maintain the anchored posture and go through the Isolation Checklist.
6. Finally, holding the anchored position, get up and walk around, letting the hands drop and allowing the arms to swing normally as you do so. (You can also locate the SCMs by raising your head from the floor one centimetre. Make sure the knees are bent and that are do not hold your breath.)

You may have noticed that I don't use imagery much in my teaching; I only like to do so if the image fits with what is actually happening in the body. However, there's a very good image for this anchoring exercise, and you may find it useful:

7. Try to pull yourself up by the ears. Work hard, and notice which muscles come into play as you do this. You will be anchoring. Remember to keep the shoulders out of the act. Now go through the Isolation Checklist.

Anchoring makes a big difference when you are singing; to feel this more effectively you are going to compare 'relaxed' singing with anchored singing.

Exercise 2: ANCHORING THE TONE

1. Sing 'EE' [iː] on a comfortable pitch and with a neutral stance. The tone is relaxed.
2. Anchor and widen the neck as in Exercise 1, assigning an effort level to the work you are doing, on a scale of one to ten.
3. Repeat with other vowels.

   What changes did you feel and hear? Your tone may well have got louder, apparently on its own. It will also have altered in another way, perhaps sounding 'wider' or 'fuller'. This will be due to increased resonance.

Exercise 3: FACE ANCHORING 1

Before you begin this exercise, look at Diagram 2 to see where you should be feeling the work when you do face anchoring. The arrows indicate points and direction of effort.

1. Widen your nostrils as though something or somebody has caused you to sneer! Work hard, and monitor the effort by checking the sides of your nostrils with the thumb and forefinger; you should feel an expansion there.
2. Release the jaw and go through the rest of the Isolation Checklist.

Diagram 2

3. Do this again with varying degrees of 'sneer' so that you can activate the muscles more, or less, according to choice.

   By working this exercise, you are activating some of the muscles of facial expression. Sometimes these are referred to as the 'mask' of the voice. These muscles are known to enhance resonance, and when you sing with these muscles working, you will feel that the tone is more stable.

Exercise 4: FACE ANCHORING 2

Repeat Exercise 2: anchoring the tone.

1. Repeat it on all vowels and on different notes of your range.
2. Repeat it with different degrees of 'sneer'.

This face anchoring is what I think is meant by 'bringing the tone forward'.

Anchoring from the inside

Now we are working with the oral cavity: working muscles which link directly and indirectly to the larynx, and maximising resonance.

Exercise 6, Chapter 6, involved the palato pharyngeus. It is an excellent way to feel that you can anchor the tone and make it more resonant. I won't repeat the exercise; you can look it up on page 62. Practise it in different parts of your range.

The 19th century Italian singers used to talk about the sensation of *inhalare la voce* – 'breathing in the voice'. You may well have heard people say, 'Don't use so much breath; sing with the feeling of breathing in.' It can be a confusing image when we know that we sing on the out-breath. The device works probably because when we suck in, we are activating the muscles of the soft palate and are firming up soft tissue at the back of the vocal tract.

Exercise 5: INSIDE THE MOUTH; SUCKING BACK

You will need a straw for this!

1. Remind yourself of what it feels like to drink liquid through a straw; your muscles will be creating suction and your soft palate will be raised so that no liquid goes down your nose.
2. Now take the straw away and make the same action to suck in. At this stage you are neither breathing in nor out, so you won't want to hold the feeling for too long.
3. Repeat stage 2, holding the sucking mechanism in position and, notice that you *can* breathe in or out. Do not worry that your lips are protruded and your cheeks pulled in.
4. Keep this feeling of the effort inside and at the back of the mouth as you gradually open the jaw more and let go of the cheeks.
5. Sing a note in your mid-range on 'EE' [iː].
   Note the following:
   i. It's easy to hold your breath in this exercise; make sure you do not do so after stage 2;
   ii. Do not tighten the tongue; roll it around as you keep the feeling of sucking back, and then continue with the rest of the Isolation Checklist.
6. Now, as in Exercise 2, on the same note sing first relaxed, then anchored, using the feeling of sucking the straw. Notice the difference in the resonance and firmness of your tone.

I have given you a range of exercises to activate the muscles that anchor the vocal tract. Practise them. Some of them will work better for you than others; use the ones you liked first in your practice, but do try them all. You may be thinking that the anchoring requires an unnatural degree of effort. I have been careful to remind you, throughout, of the need to isolate effort when practising the anchoring; the effort should not spread to other muscles when you are doing this work. This is why you have the Isolation Checklist. As you become used to using these exercises you will find that the anchoring feels more natural, and you will be able to employ it without it being obvious on stage. It's a good idea to use a mirror sometimes to check that you are not pulling faces!

You should use anchoring anytime you want to increase volume and resonance. You can also sing very quietly with anchoring, and it will still make a difference to your sound. Anchoring will give your voice 'presence' and enable you to project. People with big voices will need a degree of anchoring all the time, say between a two and four if the top of the effort scale is ten. There are a number of voice qualities for which anchoring is useful, and in belting it is a must.

I'm sometimes asked if it dangerous to think about work in the vocal folds. I don't think it is. Any muscle in the body can be overworked if we do not pay attention; that is why we have done a number of exercises in awareness. What I do know is that trying to project by working the breath and relaxing in the larynx simply does not work. You have to work the vocal folds, the body and the breath. It's a balancing act that requires awareness on the part of you and your teacher or vocal coach.

Your airflow is an important consideration. Greater sub-glottic pressure is needed to produce loud sounds, so you will feel your abdominal wall working when you do the anchoring exercises. Students often remark that the waistband or sides of the abdominal wall expand automatically when they use the anchoring exercises, and that they notice an improvement in their breath use. In the exercises that follow I would like you to be aware of any changes in the abdominal wall as you work the anchoring muscles.

Anchoring the torso

Torso anchoring is helpful to singer-dancers. Sometimes when we are working the voice and the body very hard, we overbreathe. This is particularly the case if you are doing a high-energy dance show such as Andrew Lloyd Webber's *Cats*, or a choreographed number in Rodgers and Hammerstein's *Oklahoma!* In these situations the dancers doing the routine need far more breath for the dancing than they do for the singing, and they consequently take in too much air. In singing the breath is held back, so the dancer needs a strategy for getting rid of his or her breath at every opportunity. What is needed here are 'breathing out' exercises! In Chapter 11, I will discuss how you can use the consonants to help you get rid of the breath when you have too much. Torso anchoring also helps with over-breathing and can be used by dancers during a routine without upsetting their stance.

You will also find the torso anchoring exercises useful when you produce high-energy voice qualities or sing something very sustained. Anchoring in the torso makes you safe when you are putting heavy demands on your voice. I have consistently found that people with big voices need to use a degree of torso anchoring all the time. There is something about the sheer physicality of big voices that demands this amount of input to make a decent sound; a big voice out of control can sound awful. The consequence of this is that the singer holds back, constricts and de-voices. If you suspect you are one of these people, you should use torso anchoring as a matter of course.

The areas we are going to work are the latissimus dorsi (lats for short), pectoralis minor (pecs), and the quadratus lumborum (quads). Diagram 3 overleaf shows the lats and quads.

You might be familiar with these muscle groups if you work out in the gym; though not directly related to breathing, they will help you to hold the breath back when you are working hard with your voice and body. I have used arrows to indicate not only where you should feel the effort and its direction.

The lats are two large fan-shaped muscles starting around the lower back ribs. They fan out either side of the spine and come up underneath the shoulder blades. Probably we used these muscles in our climbing days because they attach into the top of the arms. Because they are close to the surface of the skin, they are easily felt. When you do the following exercise, you will feel work in your pecs as well as in the front of the chest; the lats and pecs will be working together. Work with a partner to help you with external monitoring.

Awareness exercise 3: THE LATS

1. Stand easily with the feet comfortably apart and the knees not locked.
2. Turn your arms in their sockets away from the body, keeping them close to you. This will fix the top of your lats.
3. Keeping the lats fixed, now pull down from underneath your shoulder blades.

   What are you feeling? At stage 2 (fixing the top of the lats) you feel a bulging, just below and in front of the armpit. You might also experience a slight lift in the sternum that is not a result of breathing in. At stage 3 (the pull down) you feel this lift more, as well as a bulging and sense of widening around the back. Again, this widening has nothing to do with either breathing in or out. Look at the arrows on the diagram overleaf to see where you should be feeling the effort.
4. Get your partner to feel the lats, spreading their hands out either side of the spine from underneath the shoulder blades.
5. Do the exercise again, really paying attention to where you can feel the work, and then release your forearms and finally the upper arm. The trick is to keep the lats switched on without the arm twist! Get your partner to give you a running commentary as you go through this.

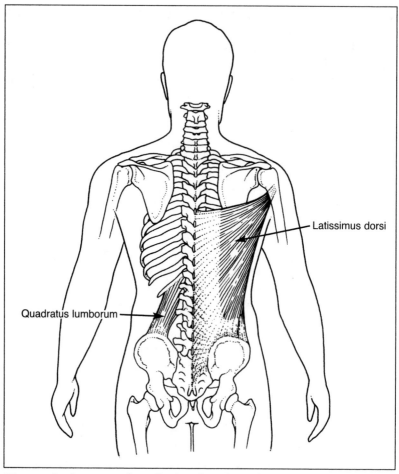

Diagram 3 – latissimus dorsi (lats) and quadratus lumborum (quads)

Later we will run this exercise again and include the Isolation Checklist (page 18). For now, do not hold your breath and notice that you can engage the lats when breathing in or out.

The quads are a pair of muscles running from the base of the spine and the back of the pelvis to your 12th ribs.

Awareness exercise 4: THE QUADS

1. Imagine you are travelling on a bus, standing up and holding on to one of those leather straps or ball-shaped holders, which are suspended from the ceiling.

2. Stand easily with the knees soft and the shoulders not tensed, even though you are reaching up with your arms.
3. As the tube or bus starts to move you want to steady yourself without locking the body. How do you do it?
4. Make sure your knees are not locked so that you can still go with the movement. You will find yourself weighting down in the pelvis and will feel work low down in the spine.

Probably you will be working both the lats and the quads in this manoeuvre. As in the previous exercise, make sure that you can breathe in and out.

You may have heard the terms 'rooting' or 'grounding' the voice; they are used more often in spoken voice teaching. I believe this is the same thing. I often hear people talk about 'being connected' when they sing. Anchoring is about how we build that sense of connection.

In broad terms, it is OK to feel your body is 'held', or braced, in the anchoring exercises, if you are feeling it around the back. At the front of the abdominal wall where you feel the recoil, it is not OK. You must always be able to breathe in or out when anchoring and this means isolation, isolation and more isolation.

Now that you know where the torso is anchored, practise singing with and without anchoring exactly as we did before for the vocal tract.

Exercise 6: WORKING THE ANCHORING WITH THE VOICE

1. Stand easily with a balanced posture and sing 'EE' [i:] on a comfortable note in your range. The dynamic level should be medium to soft.
2. Still singing, retract the false vocal folds and then suddenly anchor with the muscles of the torso. Your tone would have become more solid, possibly louder as well.
3. Repeat the sequence, this time holding the note for longer, and make a conscious effort to get softer as you sing. Notice that you can still remain anchored even when singing softly. Your breath will last for longer too.
4. Run through the Isolation Checklist.
5. If at any point you need to stop and breathe, maintain the retraction and recoil with the breath. You will find that you can maintain your anchored position. Some people like to release the anchoring altogether when they breathe in; this is OK so long as you can re-engage at the same level.
6. Repeat, going through a sequence of vowels and on different notes in your range.
7. Experiment with different positions when anchoring: standing,

walking, sitting, kneeling, lying down. This will increase your awareness and ability to isolate.

You can use any of the vocal exercises to apply the postural anchoring, for example, Exercise 3, Chapter 4 for working on sustaining, or any exercises featuring octave leaps, or ascending or descending scales. You should also be working on passages from songs. Find a phrase in a song you are working on and apply first the anchoring for the vocal tract and then the anchoring for the torso. Then apply both types of anchoring – work your body! In my experience, if you are using the torso anchoring, you will find it beneficial to anchor the head and neck as well: it will keep you in alignment. At all times monitor your effort level: you should feel work but not discomfort.

Here's a summary of what you have learned to do so far:
1. generate power from airflow;
2. close your vocal folds against the breath to create sub-glottic pressure;
3. make a wide space around the vocal folds so that they can vibrate freely;
4. manage your vocal tract to resonate;
5. provide a support structure for both the breath and the vibrating larynx.

Now you have enough knowledge to put these components together.

Exercise 7: ANCHORING THROUGHOUT YOUR RANGE

1. Start on a low note, and siren up an octave on a quiet 'ng'.
2. Still holding the top note, peel your soft palate away from the back of the tongue to make an 'EE' [iː].
3. Almost immediately, try to increase the tone by anchoring around the head, neck and face. (Use the devices that work for you.) At the same time you may also feel an increased work in the abdominal wall: the sides will be expanding laterally as you create more pressure.
   i. Make sure you have retracted the false vocal folds.

   ii. Your nasal port should be closed on the 'EE'.
   iii. Pay attention to your posture; the spine should be in alignment and

the shoulders relaxed. Your feet need to be comfortably apart at about hip width and the knees not locked.

iv. If you have done all this correctly, there will have been a dramatic increase in volume and resonance on the top note as you held it.

4. Now repeat the sequence and come back down the octave on 'EE', keeping the new dynamic level.

5. Work through your entire range like this and on all the vowels.

By now you should be having less trouble with cracks and breaks in the voice. You may find, however, that they return when you are carrying out a number of tasks at once. This is normal: singing requires a great deal of co-ordination and concentration. If your register break has come back, you are probably not retracting hard enough in the larynx. Increase your effort level in the silent laugh.

Do not go faster than thinking speed to begin with. It doesn't matter how slowly you do Exercise 7, or how many times you need to stop to think about what you are doing. Once you are sure of what you are doing you can increase your working speed. Keep this in mind as you work through the rest of the chapter.

WORKING THE RANGE

Exercise 7 was the first in which I have asked you to work through your whole range, i.e. from top to bottom. Do not be surprised if you find this difficult at first. Your voice will not feel the same all the way through and you will need to make adjustments as you work through your 'vocal keyboard'. There are usually two register changes to negotiate in the voice. You may hear them referred to as pitch breaks, gear changes, or passaggii. The cause for each change is different, and so is the solution.

Register changes: ascending the scale, first passaggio

As you ascend the scale, you may feel that you are beginning to push your voice. At some point the vocal folds need to thin their mass so that they can vibrate faster. They may also become longer at this point. (This appears to be the case as far as we understand it at the moment.) The first change of registration occurs around middle E and F (330 and 349 hertz respectively). In the female voice this is roughly one-third of the way through the range; in the male, roughly two-thirds. Note that if you are a true bass or a low mezzo, you may well experience this change two or three notes earlier, i.e. around middle C or D.

If you are having difficulty with this change point in your range:

1. Tilt the thyroid a little to allow the vocal folds to thin (see page 25).

2. Increase the work you are doing to anchor so that you do not lose volume. You should then be able to maintain a stable dynamic.

It's important that you do make an adjustment when you reach this point in your range. If you do not, you will be in danger of pushing your voice.

Ascending the scale, second passaggio

The reason for breaks at the second passaggio is different, and it's important to understand this. As you approach the top third of your range, the larynx needs to rise. So does the soft palate. Unfortunately the palato pharyngeus muscle, which is active in raising the larynx, can also lower the palate if the latter is not fixed by the levator palatini. The nasal port will then open and the sound will become thin and pinched. Some singers will feel a lot of discomfort at this point; it is not uncommon to feel that the voice is blocked because of the constriction that results from this difficulty. What's the solution?

1. Keep the nasal port closed. Review the work we did in Exercise 6, Chapter 6, on the nasal port to make a strong seal between the nose and mouth.

2. Make sure that you are allowing the larynx to rise. Review Awareness exercise 3, Chapter 3, on raising and lowering the larynx.

3. Sing the notes you are having difficulty with to 'ng-gEE' [ŋgiː] to get the muscles into position for the high notes.

Descending the scale; increasing fold mass

When you are descending the scale, you may lose power if you do not increase you vocal fold mass. The vocal folds need to be thicker on low notes if you want to maintain volume. Your vocal folds are thick when you do a glottal onset.

1. Stop singing as you approach the bottom notes, and say 'EE' [iː], using a glottal onset.

2. Then sing the pitch you were aiming for on the 'EE', still using the glottal onset.

3. Try to incorporate the same level of effort in your vocal folds as you sing the bottom of the octave again in the exercise. Remember to stay anchored. Once you have the effort level right in the vocal folds and can

remember the muscle sensation, you do not have to continue with the glottal onset. Just be aware that your fold mass has changed.

(Later in the book, I will show you how to use twang as an option for fixing this difficulty.)

Descending the scale; lowering the larynx

This is a less common problem than the register change described above. However, some students do have difficulty accessing the lowest notes of their range because they do not allow the larynx to lower. You should review Awareness exercise 3, Chapter 3, if you think this is relevant to you. Make sure that when you do lower the larynx you do not also lower the palate, as this will cause you to lose volume when the port is opened.

Changes in breath use

Contrary to popular belief, you need less air for top notes. When the vocal folds are opening and closing very fast, too much air will push them apart. You will find you need less air for top notes. The converse is true for the bottom of your range; your airflow will be greater when you sing the bottom notes.

Stage-fright and adrenalin

The larynx is suspended inside the neck, not attached directly to the spine at any point. This enables it to move up and down easily for its primary functions, but also makes it a very vulnerable mechanism. The larynx is very responsive to changes in the body: to posture, to airflow, and to our levels of adrenaline. When we are nervous the larynx is one of the first places to show it. You will find anchoring a great help in these situations. Next time you have an audition and are waiting to sing, silently go through the anchoring exercises and do the occasional siren. You will find that your voice stays 'warm' while you are waiting. Retract the false vocal folds by silently laughing from time to time to release constriction.

Wobble is an extreme form of vibrato that unfortunately is heard all too often in singers who are not anchoring hard enough. If you are singing at volume and air is pushing up against the larynx, the whole mechanism can go into shake as it tries to resist the breath. It's usually more noticeable on long, held notes where the singer has relaxed into the note, having started it. Vibrato on a note is fine, so long as it is your choice to make it. However, wobble is not. If you have a wobble, practise singing long notes with the anchoring muscles engaged and hold the effort throughout the note.

Dynamic control

The 18th and 19th century Italian singers used to work an exercise called the Messa di Voce. Essentially it is an exercise in getting louder and quieter. Musically it's depicted by the hairpins:

I like to call this increasing and decreasing the tone because there is increased work at the larynx when we sing louder, as well as in the body and breath.

Exercise 8: GETTING LOUDER AND QUIETER

1. Sing quietly on 'ng' [ŋ].
2. Still singing quietly, peel your soft palate away from the tongue: 'ng-EE' [ŋiː].
3. Anchor the vocal tract as you increase the tone (straighten the cervical spine, sneer, and widen at the neck).
4. Anchor the torso as you increase the tone further. Keep laughing silently at the larynx.
   When you first increase the tone, pay attention to the abdominals. You will need more airflow and more pressure, so there will be movement inwards at the navel and outwards at the sides.
5. Reverse the process. Still singing 'EE' [iː], reduce the effort level at the vocal folds so that you decrease the tone.
6. Keep some effort in the anchoring muscles and maintain the silent laugh. Notice that as you get quieter, you are using less air and working with the anchoring muscles to hold the air back.

If you can do this, you have mastered dynamic control!

Problem-solving with anchoring

It's difficult to give specific advice for anchoring because the needs of each voice are different. A passage that one person finds difficult in a song may be relatively easy to another. This is where the issue of vocal effort comes in; you need to know where to work harder if a passage of music is giving you difficulty, and this may be quite different for someone else. So stop and ask yourself the following questions:

1. Am I making the pitch correctly? Do I need to increase or decrease effort at vocal fold level?

2. Is there constriction at the larynx? Do I need to work harder in my retraction?

3. Do I need to increase my airflow?

4. Could I solve this problem by maximising resonance?

5. Do I need to be working harder in the body?

With these points in mind, you might find it useful to look at a song that has caused you problems in the past. Perhaps there is a song with a difficult passage in it where you tend to lose power, or where you always end up pushing the voice and cracking. These would be typical places where applying the anchoring would make a difference.

There isn't space here for me to write about every situation in which anchoring is helpful or necessary. Using a few well-known difficult passages of music from *Miss Saigon* and *West Side Story*, which you might want to learn or re-examine, I'm going to show you how anchoring can make a difference in belting and in lyric singing. Even if you do not know these pieces, or feel that none of them is suited to your voice type, you will at least get an idea of the kind of situation in which anchoring is applicable. You can then choose material of your own to practise the anchoring.

Anchoring when belting

Song assignment 1: IT'S HER OR ME – ELLEN (MISS SAIGON)

Consider the final passage starting from 'Now that I've seen her' up to 'Now I have to know'. This is a dramatic turning point in both the show and in Ellen's own story: she knows that her marriage depends on her finding out the truth of her husband's past.

You will usually need to be anchored for rising passages of music, particularly those requiring belt. In this instance, you are using the anchoring not to get louder (you are singing a rising phrase so an increase in volume is not necessary), but to stabilise your instrument as you sing a difficult passage. Usually you will be required to stay in belt during this phrase and not to flip into another voice quality. I find that most people attempting this number have no difficulty staying in belt voice up to the C or D, but are apt to crack on the upper E. I'm not going to examine the set-up for belting at this point, but if your belt is usually OK, and you are having the problem I've described in singing this song, you should try anchoring.

When we sing a rising phrase, we are asking our voice to work progressively harder because the vocal folds must vibrate faster for the higher pitches. It's important that at this point you do not drive the voice, but give support to the work in the vocal folds by using the anchoring. This is an example of an 'effort issue': where do you put the extra effort if not in the vocal folds, which are already working harder anyway? Please note that increasing airflow will not solve this problem; you would be in danger of singing sharp if you did this, and you would be asking your vocal folds to work even harder by giving them more air to resist!

Here's what you should do:

1. Start by checking that you are making the pitches correctly and without constriction. Siren the passage. Then miren it. Notice that the larynx needs to rise as you approach the upper E ('He's the one that I always trusted').
2. Still mirening, anchor the vocal tract. Check that your neck is anchored at the back and that the SCMs are engaged at the front.
3. Sing the passage to see if the work you have done has made a difference.
4. Now anchor the torso. This time, sing the passage silently as you mouth the words and breathe out as if you were singing. Notice that even doing this silent singing takes effort.
5. As you sing 'I know why he lied', anchor hard in the torso and stay anchored to the end of the song. Don't be surprised if your airflow is held back. This is actually what is needed at this point. However, you should still be able to do a recoil breath after 'lied', and again after 'trusted'. Notice the change of effort levels in the body even though you are continuing to sing silently to the end of the song. Give the feeling an effort number on a scale of one to ten.
6. Now sing the passage in full voice, with all the anchoring in place.

This should have helped. When you have learned the exercises for medialising the vowels and for twang, you will have additional strategies you could use to deal with this passage. For now, notice the difference that the anchoring made, and explore where you need to bring it in. Remember that the perception of effort is up to *you*, not your teacher or vocal coach. We can only make suggestions.

Song assignment 2: WHY GOD? – CHRIS (MISS SAIGON)

Look at the final section of this song starting at 'Why God, why this face?' and on to the end.

Chris has just had an intense emotional experience, all the more shocking to him because as a soldier he has had to cut himself off from emotional responses in order to function. The end of the song does not bring resolution to his dilemma, he is still struggling to make sense of the experience with the final phrases.

It's very easy to get tired in this passage. It has already come before in the song and the tessitura is high. Even if the high G's come easily to you, this will be a taxing piece because it is not appropriate to sing lyrically here. This is an instance where the male voice uses belt, and it is high enough for either a tenor or high baritone to belt. (See Chapter 12 for belt voice range.)

1. Sing the whole song. It is very demanding and you will need vocal stamina. Where do you think your problems lie in the song? Are you pitching correctly? Are you constricting at the larynx? Do you need to retract more? Do you need to increase your airflow? Should you be working harder in the body?

2. Now work the final passage. Siren it. Then miren it.

3. This is a high passage, and your larynx will need to be high. You are also in the second passaggio, so you will need to check that your nasal port is properly closed. If it is not closed you may not be able to get full vocal fold closure because of the difficulties with airflow and an open port. This is the most common problem I meet when working on this song (apart from constriction), and it is no good anchoring if the vocal folds are not closing properly. Practise singing '"ngy" [ŋaɪ] God' instead of 'Why God' as this will enable you to close the port and raise the larynx. When you go back to singing 'w', notice if you are lowering the larynx: it can be a problem with this consonant. (See Chapter 11 for a more detailed explanation.)

4. Do not blow air at the beginning of the phrase. Practise the attack on the first note with the anchoring switched on and using less breath.

5. The biggest difficulty arises when you sing 'remembr'ing her, just her'. This is because of the 'h' which can cause you to blow too much air through the vocal folds, forcing them apart. Practise singing this last phrase fully anchored and substitute 'y' [j] for the 'h'. This will help keep your tongue high (see Chapter 8 for more details) and help you to stop blowing air as you onset the note.

6. Check your posture at this point: is your neck wide? Is your torso anchored – not just the lats and the pecs, but also the quads?

7. The 'j' [dʒ] can give you problems because in speech we pitch it low. Practise pitching the beginning of the word just on the high G. You don't have to do this in full voice; simply voice the 'j' on the correct pitch. This will enable you to keep the larynx in its optimum position for this note.

8. If you are running out of steam at the end of the song you can take a recoil breath on the final 't' of 'just'. Make sure you stay anchored when you do the recoil because you do not have time to relax muscles other than the abdominal wall at this point.

As you can see, there are many points of vocal production to consider here if you are having difficulty singing this passage. I hope I have been able to give you some useful insights.

Anchoring with lyric singing

Anchoring is needed for intensity in lyric singing. If you are having to sing the part of either Maria or Tony in the duet *'Tonight'*, you need to be able to sustain long phrases that lead slowly to a 'money note' at the end of the sequence.

Song assignment 3: THE BALCONY SCENE (TONIGHT) – TONY AND MARIA (WEST SIDE STORY)

Women should start at the beginning of the sequence 'Tonight, tonight' and finish on 'And what was just a world is a star, Tonight', on a high F marked fortissimo. Men should start at 'Always you, every thought I'll ever know', and end of 'You and me'. On the way there is a high G that starts piano (soft) and must end forte (loud).

1. Sing the passage. Remember that you are not belting; check that you are singing with a tilted thyroid. (See Chapter 3, and also Chapter 12 for Cry quality.)
2. Siren and miren the passage, paying attention to maintaining the tilted thyroid and retraction in the larynx.
3. Still mirening, engage the vocal tract anchoring, checking yourself at front and back.
4. Pull up inside the head and behind the nose using the palato-pharyngeus muscles as we did in Exercise 6, Chapter 6. Even though you are mirening on 'ng' [ŋ] and your port is open, you will experience an extra lift around the palate and feel as though you have made a new space deep inside the head. Give this feeling an effort number.
5. Now sing the passage with the words, keeping the anchoring in place. The sound will have improved dramatically.
6. If you are having difficulty sustaining the long phrases, use a degree of torso anchoring to hold the breath back. Make sure that you recoil properly in the centre of your abdominal wall when you do take a breath.
7. You have many opportunities for breathing on the consonants in this sequence. Try breathing on the final 't' each time you say 'tonight' for instance. (See Chapter 13 for a more detailed explanation of breathing on the consonants.) If you are retracted and maintain your anchored posture, nobody will hear this as a break in the phrase. (In any case, most times this word appears, there is a comma after it, which you should acknowledge.)

8. When you have a word to hold on a long note e.g. 'world', 'night', try travelling through all the sounds in the word 'wERld' [wɜːrld] and 'nayt' [naɪt] as you sing it, rather than holding just one vowel sound for the majority of the note value. You will conserve energy this way, and be more interesting to listen to!

There's a popular school of thought amongst actors today that in order to convey reality one must be natural and relaxed. I do not share this view: there is a world of difference between conveying emotions with truth (getting the audience to feel) and in being natural, particularly on stage. We do not, in any case 'naturally' burst into song when we are dying or declaring feelings to a loved one (two of the classic cues for a song). Singing, which involves sustaining pitch, is heightened text and, as such, will be conveyed in a heightened manner. If you know how to move on stage, can react and truly wish to communicate with the audience, these exercises will only enhance what you do.

There has been a lot to learn in this chapter and a lot to put together. If you read up to this point at one go I wouldn't blame you if you put the book down feeling that the whole business was hopelessly complicated. Singing does require a high degree of co-ordination. With practice at doing each of the tasks in isolation, you can learn the co-ordination quite quickly. In the hands of a good teacher, this can happen over a matter of weeks.

Chapter 8

Tuning the oral resonator

Have you ever noticed how many people have difficulty singing the vowel 'AH' [ɑː]? No matter how wide the jaw and how flat the tongue, the 'AH' doesn't seem to get better. There's a very good reason for this: 'EE' [iː] is much easier to sing than 'AH'. 'EE' brings the tongue forward and away from the pharyngeal wall so that there is more space at the tongue root. Why is it then that 'AH' is so much favoured as the working vowel for many voice and singing exercises? I suggest that it is because 'AH' looks relaxed; the jaw is wide, and the tongue is lying on the floor of the mouth. The reasoning is that if we are relaxed we will sing well.

I do not subscribe to the notion that we are relaxed when we are singing, as you have probably realised by now. In singing we are playing an instrument, and that takes work. What you are going to learn from this chapter is how best to shape your sound so that it can be heard easily.

In Chapter 7 you learned how to make volume by increasing work in the vocal folds and by working the body. The oral resonator is one of our main sound shapers; by shaping the sound in the mouth we favour some harmonics and damp down others. Every time you make a vowel you are shaping the vocal tract; this involves controlling the tongue, the soft palate, the lips and the jaw. You will learn in this chapter that, since not all vowels are made equal, the singer needs to adjust how the vowels are shaped. This requires you to have excellent control of the tongue. You have already learned about control of the nasal port and soft palate in Chapter 6, so the remaining structures for this chapter will be the jaw and the lips.

The Jaw

I think the jaw is less important in singing than we are often led to believe. The main things are to get it out of the way, to learn to move it independently of the tongue, soft palate and lips, and to let the rest of the instrument do its work. Let's look at what the jaw is for, how it needs to move, and how it can cause us problems in singing.

The jaw provides the lower frame for the oral resonator. We do not sing with the jaw, yet it often causes us problems. A tense jaw can be one that is clamped, out of alignment, or one that is overworking to open. I want to look briefly at what might be behind these problems.

1. A mis-aligned jaw can have a knock-on effect on the larynx. When we look at how the jaw works, you will see how to remedy this, provided there is no physical reason for the alignment problem. Often poor head and neck alignment is the reason for difficulties with the jaw.

2. Misunderstandings about how to manage oral resonance are another common cause of jaw problems. The jaw isn't really important in sound-shaping; the tongue and soft palate are far more important.

3. Some students use the jaw as a substitute for supporting the larynx. If you have worked through the exercises for head and neck anchoring, you will find that you have a more efficient means of 'support' than the jaw.

The work we are about to do with the jaw is aimed at efficiency – finding out how to open and close the jaw without strain and making sure that the jaw, tongue and soft palate can be moved independently. As you work through the exercises for the jaw, you will gain awareness and be able to monitor you jaw use for yourself.

Just as our instinct to swallow affects how we use the muscles of the larynx for speech and singing, so does our use of the muscles meant for chewing and eating affect how we use the jaw. The jaw, or mandible, is a very heavy structure, and the muscles that work the jaw from above are of necessity very powerful, enabling us to hold the jaw closed. Our conditioning to hold the jaw closed is very strong. Even tiny babies, who have not yet learned how to resist gravity and who flop all over the place, know how to close the jaw. Perhaps this is because of the necessity to protect the body from unwanted entry, and also because of the link with feeding. So letting go of the jaw requires us to give in to gravity and relax certain innate defences. As adults, we sometimes only allow those muscles to relax when we are asleep!

Awareness exercise 1: HOW THE JAW WORKS

Let's look at how the joint of the jaw (temporo-mandibular or TMJ) works:

1. Put two fingers on the face just in front of the small flap of skin in front of each ear.
2. Slowly open your mouth. You will feel the head of the mandible under your fingers starting to move.
3. Notice how the joint moves: forward, then forward and down, and also rotating as you open your mouth. This is a complex set of movements. Do this action several times to get in touch with this forward-down-and-around feeling. Look at Diagrams 1 and 2 overleaf.

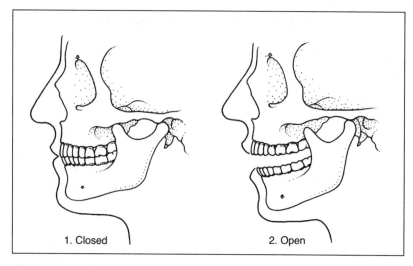

1. Closed   2. Open

The jaw in profile. Diagram 1: closed; diagram 2: open.

4. Now see if you can activate some of the other muscles that work the jaw by moving it:
   i.   side to side;
   ii. protruding (do this with the jaw bone or mandible);
   iii. down and back (as if pushing against something).

These movements are performed during chewing and eating, but not all of them are appropriate in singing.

1. An asymmetrical opening of the jaw, for instance, (involving that side to side movement) will affect your ability to resonate and also be strange to look at.

2. Pushing the jaw too far forward is a habit often associated with poor head and neck alignment. In cases of extreme forward postures, the larynx will be drawn forwards and pushed out of alignment.

3. Pushing the jaw down and back will activate supra-hyoid muscles and so exert pressure from the base of the tongue downwards onto the larynx.

These three types of jaw movement should be avoided for the purposes of singing, and the routine you practised above, encouraged.

Relaxing the jaw; isolation

Many jaw problems come about because we do not isolate sufficiently well. Remember that effort spreads in the body; in other words, when we are working hard with one or a group of muscles, we tend to bring that effort in elsewhere. This is particularly so with the jaw which likes to come in on the act of singing – when we are singing loud, singing high, forming consonants, or singing very softly – whatever the singer finds difficult. Now that you have understood how the jaw moves, all you need to do is keep checking your isolation. Every time you get to chew lazily with the jaw on the Isolation Checklist, notice how you chew.

Gravity and the jaw

Letting go the jaw is not the same as pushing it down. You cannot solve the problem of a tense jaw by pushing down with the muscles which lower the jaw. Because of the way the mechanism is set up, these muscles should only be activated if you are pushing the jaw downwards against something. Inappropriate use of these muscles can lead to tension and discomfort. A common exercise for releasing a tense jaw is to put two or three fingers' width between your front teeth. Very few people find this comfortable, and I think this exercise, rather than encouraging students to release the jaw, teaches them to engage the supra-hyoid muscles in depressing the jaw, and this will tend to push the larynx down. We do not sing *with the jaw*, and it is not necessary to sing with it wide open all the time. Some singers do have tense jaw muscles for the reasons I have given above, and will therefore need to be especially aware when doing the isolation exercises.

If you need to let go of the jaw, you should relax the muscles that are used to raise it. Because of our powerful conditioning to keep the jaw closed, this is not always easy to do, but rather than forcing the jaw to open further you should learn to give in to gravity. A functioning jaw will be able to open to two or three fingers' width, but that won't necessarily be your 'relaxed' position, so it won't be useful for singing. My own position is to aim for a relaxed jaw, paying attention to how the joint wants to move and not forcing for a larger opening. If you have pain in your jaw when you are trying to open it wider, or you feel that one side opens more than another, some physical therapy would be good: massage, osteopathy, or some kinesiology exercises. There are all kinds of reasons why the jaw may open unevenly – dentistry problems or chewing patterns are common ones – and you can sometimes need input from someone else to adjust these habitual patterns.

Awareness exercise 2: GIVING IN TO GRAVITY WITH THE JAW

Practise this with a mirror.
1. As in Awareness exercise 1, place your fingers on the small flap in front of the ears, and move the jaw slowly forward and down, giving in to gravity. At this point some muscles are working to suspend the heavy

jawbone, but you are relaxing the powerful masseter muscle. This is what we mean when we say, 'let the jaw hang'.

2. Still looking in the mirror, allow your jaw to hang in this position. Almost certainly you will not be able to get two fingers' width into your mouth at this stage.

3. Now open the jaw further. Notice that you are engaging other muscles that open the mouth: the anterior belly of the digastric, and the supra-hyoid muscles (the mylohyoid and geniohyoid). These last two are not needed in opening the jaw. Put your thumb underneath your chin to feel if you are pushing down in this area. You want to avoid this. You can probably manage two fingers' width at this stage.

4. If you go further still, you will feel the joint (just in front of the ears) pushing forward as the jaw is pulled down and back. A jaw that is held in this position during singing will inhibit free upward movement of the larynx, causing difficulties with high notes.

Awareness exercise 3: THE HANGING JAW POSITION

This exercise is useful if you have difficulty achieving the 'hanging jaw' position; it will enable you to relax somewhat the fibres of your masseter muscle.

1. Put your elbows onto a table or other suitable surface. Put your thumbs underneath the cheekbones.

    You are feeling for the muscles between the zygomatic bone (cheekbone) and maxilla (just above your top teeth) and the jawbone (mandible). There are a number of muscles here, but you will probably only get in contact with the masseter, which is closest to the surface, and the buccinator, which you actually use to stop food falling out of your mouth. Go gently at first because it's likely to be painful!

2. Work your way into the non-bony area between the cheekbone, jaw and mouth, and gradually increase the pressure by pushing up with your thumbs and letting them support the weight of your head as it drops down and forward. All the time your elbows are on the table, giving you further support.

3. As you do this, allow the jaw to drop open and feel how you can let go a little more in those muscles you are feeling.

4. Slowly bring your head up again, taking care to align yourself and leaving the jaw where it is.

This is the best exercise you can do for yourself to help relax the jaw. If you are a determined person, a worrier or a nocturnal teeth grinder, all of whom tend to jaw tension, you'll find it very useful!

Song assignment 1: YOUR SONG

Work with a partner, choosing a song that you know quite well and which involves some leaps to high and low notes. The jaw has nothing to do with pitch change, and I want your partner to give you feedback about how you use your jaw in these situations.

1. In a standing position, allow your partner to take the weight of your head as you drop it down and forward. Your partner's hands should be holding you gently around the back of the neck and supporting you from the front underneath your forehead.

2. Now let your partner slowly and gently bring your head to an upright position, keeping the neck in alignment with the rest of the spine. This is important because many people have jaw tension through not supporting their head correctly against gravity, and so feel the need to 'hold on' somewhere else.

3. Once your head is in position, use your own forefinger and thumb of both hands to encourage the jaw to give in to gravity. *Don't pull*; just hold on with the fingers at the chin and let go of the jaw.

4. Take your hands away, and start to sing the song you have chosen. Ask your partner to notice the positioning of the jaw while you are singing, not just how far you have opened, but also how far forward or back the jaw is. They can place a finger gently on the chin to remind you of this positioning while you are singing.

5. As you sing the song, notice when you need to open and close the jaw for articulating consonants, and whether you have a habit of clamping the jaw for certain vocal manoeuvres. (Common ones are pulling back the jaw for extremes of range and clamping when we don't like the sound or have a difficult passage to sing.)

6. As you continue singing your partner can continue to remind you of good jaw positioning by placing their finger on your chin, as necessary:
   i. if the jaw is pushing forward they can encourage it to go back a little;
   ii. if the jaw is tense they can encourage you to give in to gravity;
   iii. if the jaw is pulled down too far they can help you to close up a little more.

   You will probably become more aware of the work done by the palate, tongue and lips in shaping the sound when you do this exercise, and it will prepare you for the next section on the tongue. At all times your articulation should be clear, with correct vowel formation and crisp consonants.

Jaw shake is a rather distressing phenomenon that we see from time to time in singers. The reason for it is this: your voice is a vibrating mechanism, and when you are producing high-energy sounds this mechanism has to offer some resistance to the oncoming airflow.

Resistance in the vocal folds alone is not enough (see Chapter 7), and there must be support around the larynx so that the whole vocal tract does not vibrate in sympathy with it. Your jaw is at the front end of the vocal tract, and when it shakes it means that you are either too relaxed, or that you are tensing the jaw as a substitute for support. In either case, postural anchoring of the head, neck and face will stop the shake.

What you will discover from doing the previous exercises is that, provided there are no physical problems with the mechanism of the jaw, it really isn't very active in singing.

THE TONGUE

'Make your mouth space like the inside of a cathedral!' This instruction was given to a student of mine by a previous singing teacher in order to improve oral resonance. It seems logical: more space, more sound. In fact it produced a very dark sound, which meant that my student started to push his voice in order to get more volume. Making the mouth bigger does not make you sing louder. The source of increased volume is at the vocal folds, and you do not want to overwork them. What you *can* do is shape your vocal tract to enhance the sound to the ear of the listener: this is the only way we can amplify the sound created in the larynx. You will see how this works when we get to medialising later in the chapter, and in Chapter 9. When we start to look at the tongue and the resonating qualities of the different vowels, you'll see that bigger isn't necessarily better! Let's start by looking at Diagrams 3 and 4 showing the tongue:

Can you see how big the tongue is? What we can see inside the mouth is only about a third of the whole structure and is mostly intrinsic muscles. The other extrinsic muscles link the tongue to the jaw (at the front) to the styloid process (above and inside the head), to the hyoid bone below (remember that this is the top of the larynx), and to the soft palate and pharyngeal wall behind.

You can see that movement of the tongue can have a knock-on effect on a number of structures. In particular, it can affect the use of the last three mentioned above: the hyoid, the soft palate and the pharyngeal wall. Here are four common problems resulting from misunderstandings about tongue use. You might recognise yourself in one of them.

1. The student has been told to keep the tongue 'out of the way'. Your tongue is big; you cannot get it out of the way. If you try to do this, you will push down at the back and root of the tongue, giving you less space at the back of the pharynx. A tongue pushing downwards will interfere with movement of the larynx, and the student will usually have trouble accessing the top of the range. Medialising the vowels and raising the back of the tongue for high notes will address this problem.

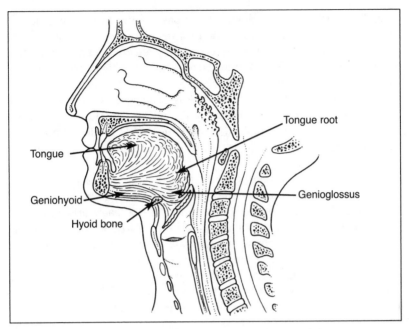

Diagram 3: sagittal section of the head indicating the size of the tongue

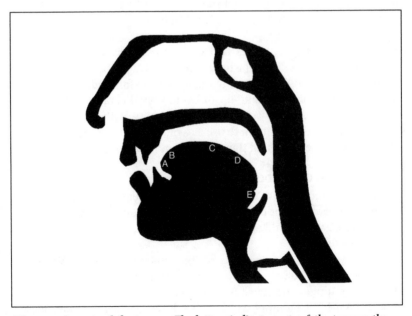

Diagram 4: parts of the tongue. The letters indicate parts of the tongue: the tip (A), blade (B), front (C), back (D), and root (E).

2. The student pushes down at the base of the tongue in order to produce a dark sound. This is OK to a degree; it will get you a dark 'covered' sound. But you will also be exerting downward pressure on the larynx, and that will give you problems with your high notes. You will also create problems with your airflow if you are depressing the tongue hard enough, due to back pressure. This is a bad plan. I find this is often a problem with singers who are trying to make a big 'chest voice': they don't understand how to make the tube longer, and they don't know how to access the thicker vocal folds needed for loud sounds at the bottom of the range.

3. Because of tongue depression the student has problems with nasality. Part of the tongue connects with the palate, causing the palate to be lowered as the tongue pushes downwards. This probably arises from an incomplete picture of 'how to make space' in the oral cavity and means that the functioning of the tongue and soft palate are not sufficiently isolated. For a solution to this problem, see the exercise below for making a good seal.

4. The singer sings well on some vowels and not others. Since each vowel makes a different shape in the vocal tract it is bound to alter the quality of your resonance. These differences are produced by changes in the tongue position and, to a lesser extent, the lips. In singing you need to adjust these changes, without distortion, so that there is no fall-off in resonance as you move through the vowels. I will give you exercises for this medialising of vowels later in this chapter.

The following exercise serves two purposes. Firstly, you will learn to engage intrinsic muscles of the tongue to raise it at the back when you are singing high. Secondly, by keeping the tongue-tip forward, you will learn to separate work at the tongue-tip and front from that of the tongue back. One of the reasons why singers have difficulty with their tongue in singing is that they are taught to use it as one unit. The tongue is made up of a number of sections and their efforts can be separated.

Exercise 1: THE TONGUE DORSUM

1. Open your mouth with a relaxed jaw, and extend the tongue. Push it right out beyond your bottom lip (unless your tongue is really short, in which case you should adjust the exercise) and, if necessary, hold onto it with a finger.
2. So that you can get used to this position, make some noises. Make sure that you are holding the silent laugh at the larynx.
3. Keep the tongue extended. Starting on an easy pitch, sing an octave leap on 'AH'. The vowel will sound a little strange, but that doesn't matter. Notice if your tongue-tip is pulling back as you go up in pitch; gently monitor the tongue-tip with your finger to prevent this.

Alternatively, you could use a mirror. If you are doing this correctly, you will notice that the back of the tongue bunches up as you slide up to the high notes. Intrinsic muscles of the tongue are engaged so that the larynx can rise for the top notes, giving you easier access to them.

4. Work your way up through your range, bringing in any other adjustments such as anchoring or thyroid tilting as you need them. Work this exercise until you can do it without discomfort.
5. Once you have reached the top of your range, start to descend, still singing on 'AH'. Gradually take your finger away (or stop watching in the mirror), and withdraw the tongue to its normal positioning inside the mouth. The back of the tongue should still be rising for the high notes.

THE TONGUE AND SOFT PALATE

If you look at the side view of the tongue again (and perhaps glance back at Diagram 5, Chapter 6), you will see that there is a muscle at the back connecting the body of the tongue with the palate. It is called the palato-glossus. If the palate isn't working efficiently and you are using your tongue to make more space at the back of the mouth, the palato-glossus could pull the palate down and lead to nasality. The following exercise will help you to maximise efficiency in your palate control and stop you using the muscles that form the floor of the mouth (one of which is the tongue) to work the oral cavity. You should remind yourself of the exercises for the palate on page 58 before attempting this:

Exercise 2: MAKING A GOOD SEAL BETWEEN THE NOSE AND MOUTH

1. Place your thumb and forefingers on the chin (as you did in the Song Assignment) so that you can monitor the tongue base and floor of the mouth while you do this exercise. Go through the palate control sequence using the vowels 'EE' [iː] to 'OO' [uː].
2. Do the work of closing the nasal port by moving the soft palate only, minimising the work you do on the floor of the mouth. You can monitor this by holding your thumb underneath the chin; you will feel some movement there on the 'EE' vowel, otherwise the movements should be small. Do the move from 'ng' [ŋ] to each vowel fairly slowly at first so that you have thinking and feeling time. Then you can increase speed.
3. Once you have got this working well you can start to use more voice and sustain the vowels for longer. If you can apply the anchoring muscles which are deep to the palate (remember the muscles deep to the palate discussed in Chapter 7?), you will create a considerable increase of tone without having to open the jaw any wider.

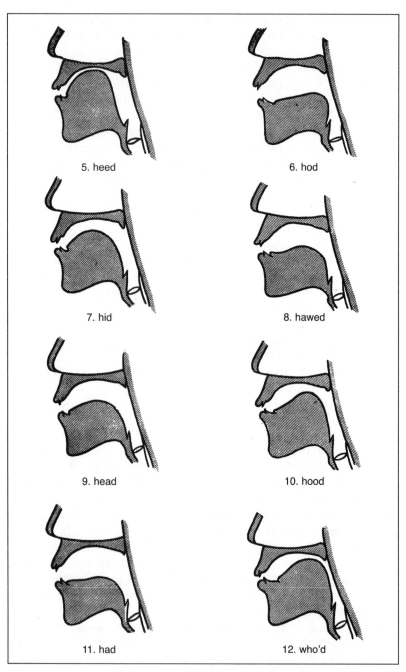

Diagrams 5 -12: the positions of the vocal organs for the words 'heed', 'hod', 'hid', 'hawed', 'head', 'hood', 'had' and 'who'd' (based on X-ray photographs).

VOWEL FORMATION

In working this section, I advise you to use the vowel keys on pages 45-47. The interpretative spellings for phonetic symbols are different in some cases for British and American speech. If you don't read phonetics you will need the charts.

Let's consider how we form the vowels. Look at Diagrams 5-12 opposite of eight simple vowels (reproduced from P Ladefoged's *Elements of Acoustic Phonetics*, University of Chicago Press, 1962).

Why do so many people have difficulty singing the vowel 'AH'? I began this chapter by commenting on this phenomenon, and now I'll answer the question. Not all vowels are made equal. Since the shape of the vocal tract alters with each of the vowels, the resonance also changes. This, of course, is how we differentiate between the vowels: each of them has their own pattern of harmonics. In singing, this can create difficulties. We need to sustain pitch in singing and do not want a noticeable fall-off in resonance between syllables when we are trying to project in a theatre space. Because of the way we hear sound, the front vowels are heard more easily in a large space than the back vowels, and singers are usually conscious of this, which leads them to modify their vowels.

What can we do to address this, without turning all our vowels into a version of whichever we find easiest to sing? I hope you know what I mean by this. If you listen to an opera singer singing musical theatre or a jazz standard, you will get the idea: the vowel sounds can be all wrong because the singer is actually producing Italian vowels. (Happily this is a situation that is improving in so-called crossover singing.) And it is not only classical singers who modify the vowels in order to sound more 'beautiful' or resonant. It is part of received teaching. I often see a music score with the instruction 'sing "AH"' written over any notes above the stave, so that the top note is easier to sing. Some mezzo-sopranos and baritones who are trying to develop richness in their voices sing everything as a version of 'AW' [ɔː] because the larynx is often lowered with this vowel making the vocal tract is longer.

I would like to offer an alternative solution to this difficulty which faces singers – a solution that involves tuning the vocal tract to its most resonant position while keeping the vowels intact. It's called medialisation.

Medialisation

When defining vowel placement, we look at where the vowels are formed in the mouth space: *front* (near the lips and teeth) to *back* (near the throat), and *close* (near to the roof of the mouth) and *open* (near the floor of the mouth). Hence each vowel is defined as:

1. front, central or back (and all the gradations in-between);
2. close, mid or open (and all the gradations in-between).

Look at Diagram 13 below.

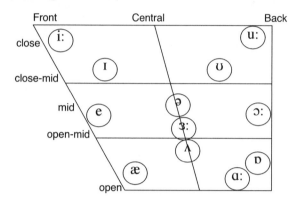

Diagram 13: vowel chart representing the divisions of the mouth space.

These are standard vowel placements as defined by the International Phonetic Association. Included in the chart are all the simple vowels of Standard British speech. If you glance at Diagrams 14 and 15 you will see how this chart fits into the mouth.

Medialising involves a change of placement for the vowels. It means closer tongue and fronting the vowel. That is, *the tongue is closer to the roof of the mouth, and the vowel is made nearer the front of the mouth.*

Look at Diagrams 14 and 15 showing the placement in the mouth for the vowel 'AH' [ɑː], where the tongue is in its most open position, i.e. lying on the floor of the mouth:

Diagram 14 shows the usual positioning. Notice the narrow distance between the back of the tongue and the back wall of the pharynx.

Diagram 14: 'AH' [ɑː]   *Diagram 15: medialised 'AH' [ɑː]*

Diagram 15 shows the same vowel with medialisation. Notice that the tongue body is now raised and advanced, and that what was a narrow distance between the back of the tongue and the wall of the pharynx is now widened. The root of the tongue is no longer covering the sound coming up from the larynx.

What are the advantages of this medialising?

1. By changing the relationship between the back of the tongue, the roof of the mouth and the back wall of the pharynx, you have put your instrument into a more favourable position for making a good sound that is shaped to the ear of the audience.

2. By keeping the tongue-tip behind the bottom front teeth, you will find it easier to differentiate activity between the front and back of the tongue.

3. Something else happens that is not shown in the diagrams above: the tongue is spread at the sides, such that it is positioned on the upper back molars. This spreading of the tongue serves a dual purpose:

i. It enables you to feel that the tongue is positioned correctly, directing the tongue's effort onto the teeth;

ii. It allows for a funnelling of resonance.

Please note that the nasal port should be closed for all vowels.

You might wonder if you were changing the vowels by doing this: you would be if you weren't doing it for all the vowels because the relationship between them would be distorted. If you look at the vowel boxes in Diagrams 16-21 overleaf, you will see that in the medialised position, although the box is further forward in the mouth cavity, the relationship between the vowels remains the same. The ear will compute this in listening and will hear the vowels as correct. You will find that the effect of medialising is far more dramatic in the back and mid-vowels: 'OO' [uː], 'AW' [ɔː], 'aw' [ɒ], 'AH' [ɑː] and 'ER' [ɜː]. The front vowels 'EE' [iː], 'eh' [e] and 'ae' [æ] do not require any change unless you are not forming them correctly. Some singers change the vowel shapes in order to create more space in the mouth, thinking that bigger is better. Medialising the vowels will correct this problem.

Note that the port is closed for all these vowels. You cannot see from the pictures that the sides of the back of the tongue are touching the molars.

You might ask if your tongue is up at the back and at the sides, how you can do anything. Actually you can do a lot with your tongue in this position. Even with the sides up, the middle of the tongue can still cup and arch: this is how we make the differences between the vowels in medialising. All sounds in Standard British and American are median except for 'l' and 'll' which are lateral: the flipped, clear 'l' [l] (as in last), and the held, dark 'll' [ɫ] (as in 'pull'). That is to say, they are defined by what happens across the middle section of the tongue from front to back; as you

Diagram 16: [uː] as in 'shoes'

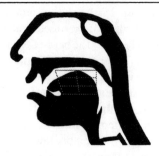

Diagram 17: medialised [uː]

Diagram 18: [ɔː] as in 'horse'

Diagram 19: medialised [ɔː]

Diagram 20: [ɒ] as in 'soft'

Diagram 21: medialised [ɒ]

make the sound, the airstream is moving across the middle of the tongue. So there should be no problem in articulating all the vowels and consonants with medialisation.

Diagram 16: [uː] as in 'shoes'. The lips are protruded and the space between the tongue and pharynx is narrow.

Diagram 17: medialised [uː]. The sides of the back of the tongue are on the molars. Note the increased space behind the back of the tongue into the pharynx. The port is closed.

Diagram 18: [ɔː] as in 'horse' (U.S first sound only). The lips are protruded and the space between the tongue and pharynx is narrow.

Diagram 19: medialised [ɔː]. Note the increased space between tongue and pharynx. The lips are still protruded.

Diagram 20: [ɒ] as in 'soft'. The tip of the tongue is not directly behind the bottom front teeth. The lips are protruded, and the space between the tongue and pharynx is narrow.

Diagram 21: medialised [ɒ]. The tip of the tongue is now behind the bottom front teeth. The body of the tongue is now slightly raised and advanced. The space between the tongue and pharynx is now increased.

Getting ready to medialise

In Standard British vowel placement, the neutral position is 'er' [ə]. You can see this in the middle of the vowel chart on page 106. In medialising, the base position, which I will call 'ready position', is 'EE' [iː].

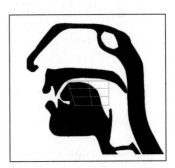

Diagram 22: [iː] the 'ready' position

The 'EE' is placed as far forward as possible and is close to (though not touching) the palate. The tip of the tongue is behind the bottom front teeth. This brings the whole body of the tongue closer to the front, thus away from the back wall of the pharynx. This is a working position for the tongue, not a neutral one. When you are getting ready to sing, neutral is not enough.

Exercise 3: MEDIALISING – STAGE I

1. Raise the back of the tongue by saying 'EEng' [iːŋ]. Now spread the tongue at the back until you can feel teeth (the upper back molars) with your tongue.
2. Stop and register all that you have done.
3. Start the exercise again, getting into the ready position by raising and spreading the back of the tongue.
4. You are now in position to do the next sound which is a union of two sounds in English: 'n' and 'y' [j]. It is the palatal nasal 'NY' [ɲ]; you

Diagram 23: [ɲ]. (Note the wide space between the tongue and the back wall of the pharynx. The port is half-open. The body of the tongue is raised and advanced. The arrows indicate the direction of sound.)

make this sound when you say the words 'vignette' or 'gnocchi'. Look at Diagram 23 to see how this looks in the vocal tract.

You will notice that the port is slightly open when you make this sound. This is the practice sound that enables you to prepare for medialising. Later you will close the port as you do the vowels.

5. Now say very slowly: 'nnyEE' – 'nnyeh' – 'nnyAH' – 'nnyAW' – 'nnyOO' [ɲjiː] – [ɲje] – [ɲjɑː] – [ɲjɔː] – [ɲjuː].

i. Close the nasal port as you go into the vowel each time.

ii. Take a breath anytime you need it.

iii.Round your lips on 'AW' [ɔː] and 'OO' [uː] as usual.

It's important that, as you move from the 'n' part of the sound to the 'y' part, you spend time on the transition point, which is the 'y'. I want you to emphasise the 'y'; this will close the nasal port and keep the back of the tongue moving forward.

What did you notice? There is a dramatic change of positioning for the 'AH' vowel, but it now matches the brightness and resonance of the 'EE'. *In fact, you were able to make all the vowels equally bright.* The back vowels will also feel easier to make because the sound is not being trapped between the tongue root and the pharyngeal wall. You are shaping the oral resonator to the ear of the listener, which means you will be heard more easily.

Look out for the following:

i. There are still minor adjustments to make from vowel to vowel. You can feel more of the teeth in some vowels than in others; this is OK so long as the sides of the tongue maintains some contact with the back molars.

ii. As you move from the 'NY' [ɲ] into the vowel you will close the port and feel the front of the tongue moving forward. This is correct.

iii. If you are not used to doing this, it will feel like work. Go through your Isolation Checklist paying particular attention to the jaw, which should not be clamped. (You won't of course be rolling the tongue around in your mouth.)

Exercise 4: MEDIALISING – STAGE 2

You should be aiming now to keep the tongue in its raised, widened position, but without the 'NY' [ɲ].

1. Start in the ready position, and sing only the first vowel with the 'NY' as preparation.

'NY' – 'EE' – 'eh' – 'AH' – 'AW' – 'OO'

[ɲ] – [iː] – [e] – [ɑː] – [ɔː] – [uː].

2. Make the changes from one vowel to the next slowly at first, and then gradually build speed.
3. Now do the whole sequence only on vowels using different notes in your range.
4. On a descending scale go through pairs of vowels on the same note, always starting with 'EE'. Work in all the simple vowels from the chart overleaf, using the vowel box on page 100 as a reference point.

'EE'–'eh' 'EE'–'AH' 'EE'–'AW' 'EE'–'OO'

[iː]–[e] [iː]–[ɑː] [iː]–[ɔː] [iː]–[uː]

You can work through your entire range in this way and will soon find that there is no change in resonance and energy as you go from one vowel to another.

Song assignment 2: ANYONE CAN WHISTLE; YOUR SONG

We are going to pinpoint a problem area and apply the principles of vowel medialisation. Consider the following phrase in Sondheim's *'Anyone Can Whistle'*.

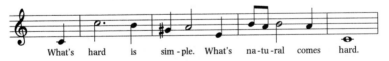

What's hard is sim - ple. What's na-tu-ral comes hard.

There is an 'AH' [ɑː] vowel on a high note, and you may well have difficulty with it because you are flattening and depressing the tongue.

1. Sing the top note on 'hEE' [hiː] then 'hyAH' [hjɑː], keeping the tongue close to the hard palate. When you do this exercise for the first time, you may find that you sing sharp on the top note. This will be because you have been used to the 'AH' sounding dark and have tried to compensate by adjusting the pitch very slightly. Alternatively you were pushing air through the 'AH', and that would have caused you to go

Standard British Vowels: Monothongs

Long vowels

[ɑ:]   open back long unrounded, as in **t**a**sk, r**a**ther, m**a**rk
[ɜ:]   mid central long unrounded, as in st**er**n, b**ir**d, t**ur**f
[ɔ:]   open mid back long rounded, as in b**o**red, w**a**lker, l**aw**
[i:]   close front long unrounded, as in sh**e**, m**ea**n, f**ee**d
[u:]   close back long rounded, as in m**o**ve, cr**u**de, b**oo**t

Short vowels

[ɪ]   close mid front short unrounded, as in k**i**d, st**i**ll, w**i**sh
[æ]   open front short unrounded, as in s**a**d, b**a**n, spl**a**sh
[e]   mid front short unrounded, as in fr**e**sh, t**e**nth, s**e**ction
[ʌ]   open mid central short unrounded, as in b**u**tton, w**o**rry,
      w**o**nder
[ɒ]   open mid back short rounded, as in wh**a**t, s**o**ft, c**o**st
[ʊ]   close mid back short rounded, as in l**oo**k, p**u**llets, p**u**t
[ə]   mid central short unrounded, as in th**e**, **a**lone, tak**e**n

Standard American Vowels: Monothongs

Long vowels

[ɑ:]   open back long unrounded, as in f**a**ther, s**o**vereign, c**a**lm
[ɝ:]   rhotic mid central long unrounded, as in p**er**fect, pref**er**,
      s**ur**geon
[ɒ:]   open mid back long rounded, as in th**aw**, wr**o**ng, s**aw**
[i:]   close front long unrounded, as in sh**e**, m**ea**n, f**ee**d
[u:]   close back long rounded, as in m**o**ve, cr**u**de, b**oo**t

Short vowels

[ɪ]   close mid front short unrounded, as in k**i**d, st**i**ll, w**i**sh
[æ]   open front short unrounded, as in s**a**d, b**a**n, spl**a**sh
[ɛ]   open mid front short unrounded, as in fr**e**sh, t**e**nth, s**e**ction
[ʌ]   open mid central short unrounded, as in w**a**s, wh**a**t, **u**nder
[ʊ]   close mid back short rounded, as in l**oo**k, p**u**llets, p**u**t
[ə]   mid central short unrounded, as in th**e**, **a**lone, tak**e**n
[ɚ]   rhotic mid central short unrounded, as in s**ur**prise,
      p**er**chance, moth**er**

(Refer to Diagram 13, page 100, to clarify placement.)

sharp. Now that you can medialise the vowels, adjust your tuning accordingly and notice that you are more voice-efficient. The principle will be exactly the same if you are singing in American; the only difference will be the use of the vowel with hard 'r' colouring, e.g. 'urr' [ɝ]. In this case, the vowel then becomes a diphthong, requiring the tongue to move. I will discuss dealing with diphthongs in Chapter 11.

2. Continue doing this with any problem vowels in any song you are learning, scrolling through the vowels to the one you need to sing, keeping the sides of the tongue high so that you can match the resonance of your 'EE' vowel.

THE LIPS

The lips form the front of the oral cavity and hence are the end point of the vocal tract. Several groups of muscles control the lips, and, together with the tongue, are needed to articulate consonants and to form some of the vowels. These muscle groups fall into five categories:

1. muscles that raise the upper lip and corners of the mouth;
2. the obicularis oris (the kissing muscle) for closing and protruding the lips;
3. muscles that depress the lower lip;
4. muscles which pull back the corners of the mouth and lips;
5. the mentalis, which enables us to protrude the lower lip and pout.

You don't need to remember all these names, but you do need both muscularity and agility in these muscle groups in order to meet the demands of good articulation. You also need to be able to separate their action from that of the jaw, in particular, and the tongue.

Lip protrusion, or rounding, is essential for the following vowels:

1. 'OO' [uː]; the lips should be well-rounded and the back of the tongue close;
2. 'ou' [ʊ] (as in book); the lips should be slightly less rounded and more open, and the back of the tongue should be mid-close;
3. 'AW' [ɔː]; the lips should still be protruded, but less rounded, and the back of the tongue open to mid;
4. 'aw' [ɒ]; the lips should be rounded but less protruded, and the back of the tongue is open.

Please note that these are the positions for the tongue before medialising. Check back to page 102 in this chapter to see the diagrams of normal and medialised positioning. In singing you will want to medialise, which means keeping the back of the tongue close and the body of the tongue fronted.

The lips are involved in the formation of the following consonants:
1. 'p', 'b' and 'm'; both lips;
2. 'f' and 'v'; lips and teeth;
3. 'w' and 'hw' [ʍ]; lips and velum.

We will deal with the work done by the lips in forming consonants in Chapters 11, 'Am I communicating?'

Exercise 5: WORKING THE LIPS

Working in front of a mirror, perform the following facial movements. Work each stage for a few minutes at a time, alternating each new posture with a neutral, relaxed expression.

1. With the lips closed, sneer. Spread the nostrils a little, and also draw the upper lip towards the nose by shortening the space between the upper lip and nose.
2. With the lips open, insert the top of your thumb between the upper and lower teeth. Try to raise the upper lip on its own. Keep the tongue and jaw relaxed. (You can insert the thumb up to the knuckle joint providing it is comfortable for you.) This will work the muscles that raise the upper lip.
3. Close the lips and smile like the 'Joker' in *Batman*. You will be working the muscles that lift the corners of the mouth.
4. Open the mouth again to the thumb-knuckle position. Take the thumb away and make fish lips like a goldfish – alternately rounding and pulling back the lips.
5. With the jaw closed, pull your mouth down in a frown. Now stick your lower lip out as if in a sulk. This sequence works the muscles that depress the lower lip.
6. To work the mentalis (the muscle which links the chin to the lips, drawing the chin up), open your jaw again and try to make your chin quiver like a crying child. Your lower lip should still protrude.
7. With the jaw closed, smile; make a wide-spread smile that flattens into your face. Then smile very smugly, this time keeping the corners of your mouth in. You are now working the muscles that pull back the corners of the mouth.

Work these exercises for a few minutes at a time, alternating each new posture with a neutral, relaxed expression.

In Chapter 3, we discovered that the larynx can lower and rise, which will make the vocal tract tube longer or shorter. You can also adjust your vocal tract length with the lips. Try this exercise.

Exercise 6: LENGTHENING THE VOCAL TRACT WITH THE LIPS

1. Sing on the vowel 'EE' with the lips relaxed first and then protruded. Notice that the sound becomes slightly darker; if you go far enough forward in the lips, you will be singing the French vowel 'u' [y].
2. Try this with any of the vowels that are normally made with the lips relaxed. Notice that there is quite a change in vocal colour.
3. Now do the opposite, i.e. sing on 'AH' [ɑː] and pull the lips back. You will shorten the vocal tract a little and the sound will become brighter.

There are schools of thought in favour of both these techniques: singing with slightly protruded lips and singing with smiling lips. In fact, you can use these features to change the sound during long held notes, changing from a brighter to a more muted tone, and vice-versa.

Song assignment 3: YOUR SONG

Choose a song that has presented you with difficulties in the past.
1. It may have a difficult approach to a high note on which you have previously been pushing the tongue down. You can now correct this using the exercises for the tongue root and tongue base. Allow the larynx to rise as part of your preparation for the top note.
2. The song may have a passage in it that never seems to sound good in your voice. This may be a part of your vocal range that just isn't very resonant (remember that the vocal tract acts as filter for the harmonics which are amplified in resonance: it enhances some and dampens down others), and you may be able to correct this by adjusting the tongue. Do the exercise for medialising the vowels in this difficult passage and see if it makes a difference. Make sure that you are retracted and not pushing air; when we have a difficult patch in our voice we often constrict in the larynx and/or push air to compensate for the lack of resonance. Again, this should correct itself if you use medialisation.

This has been a lengthy chapter, yet we still haven't covered all the work that goes on in the oral cavity! I have concentrated almost solely on the mouth as a sound-shaper rather than an articulator. In singing we are playing an instrument, and it's important to know how to adjust all the different parts. The articulation of consonants is a large topic. I will be covering this in Chapters 11 and 13 that deal with the working of text.

Chapter 9

Twang

So far we have done quite a lot of work on resonance: Chapter 6 was about controlling the nasal port, hence making a choice between oral and nasal resonance; Chapter 8 was about tuning the oral resonator. Before we move on to twang, which is advanced resonance work, let's consider the following concepts about sound-making.

1. The power for our sound is generated by breath.

2. The sound source is produced in the larynx by the vibration of the vocal folds.

3. The sound is then modified:

i. In the vocal tract;

ii. By the ears of the listener;

iii. By the space we are working in (I include in this work done by the sound engineer).

Most actors are aware of maybe the first and certainly the third of these options for modification. What we tend not to take into account is the second: how the human ear hears. When we use twang, we are using the acoustic properties of the vocal tract and the perceptual properties of the human ear.

In Chapter 1, I explained that when we sing a note it is not just one pitch or frequency that we are making. Any pitched sound produces a range of frequencies that are called harmonics. The pitch is named by the first harmonic or fundamental frequency. Here's a reminder of the harmonics you get from bass bottom C:

Each instrument has a different shape. The harmonic series for the pitch or fundamental frequency is always the same, but the shape of the instrument will enhance some harmonics and damp down others. In this way, your instrument acts as a sound filter. This is how the human ear computes the difference between one instrument and another. Your vocal tract is a tube that has its own resonating frequency: this is what makes it unique. It's also one of the things that may determine whether you sing bass or tenor, mezzo-soprano or soprano. But the voice is more complex and versatile than is implied by these categories; it can change its shape, and this will alter the patterning of the harmonics. We call this 'changing voice quality'.

When we sing a pitch, the vocal tract shapes itself and the harmonics group themselves in clusters. Each cluster has a peak, and these peaks in singing voice are called 'formants'. The formants are really a way of measuring what is going on as we resonate in the vocal tract. In Chapter 8 we looked at the different shapes made in the vocal tract by the standard vowel sounds. The patterning of harmonics is different for each vowel, and this is how we can identify the vowel sounds. Because the human ear hears certain groups of harmonics more easily than others, we altered the patterning slightly by medialising the vowels, so that the front and back vowels would be heard as equally loud. We can also make adjustments by raising or lowering the larynx – making the vocal tract longer or shorter – and by using 'twang'.

The human ear canal also has its own resonating frequency. When it hears this range of pitches, it resonates in sympathy with them. These notes are too high to sing as pitch (they are at the top end of the piano); however, they are present in every note we sing as harmonics, and it is possible to boost these harmonics using twang. What's the advantage? When the ear hears twang, it comes out to meet you. The result is that you will sound louder!

THE SINGER'S FORMANT AND TWANG

The resonating frequency band for the outer canal of the ear ranges between 2,500 and 4,000 hertz. This is what we boost when using twang. Because of the advantage this gives to singers – enabling them to be heard above a full orchestra without amplification – this band of harmonics has been called the singer's formant. Singers are not the only professional voice users who employ twang: trained actors also use it to fill a big space, drill sergeants, street hawkers and newspaper sellers use it too.

Twang in its pure form is bright, brassy and not particularly pleasant. When you hear a voice carrying above the noise of the Underground and wish that that person would shut up, that is twang! The famous comedian, Kenneth Williams, sometimes used pure twang to create a burlesque, or even and irritating effect, in performance, and the

Australian comedian Barry Humphries uses it to boost the uppermost range of his voice as Dame Edna Everidge.

You will recognise twang as a component of the Broadway and British musical theatre sound. It is also a component of fine operatic singing, which the Italians call 'squillo'. Pavarotti definitely has twang! You can use twang in its pure form, but it is fairly strident and therefore probably only suitable for character voices or moments in extremis. It is more usual to mix twang with other voice qualities in your singing to boost the sound levels. You will find twang invaluable as a vocal colour and volume booster. You cannot fill a large acoustic space without twang, and you will not be able to rely on your voice carrying above the band if you don't have it. The sound man is usually very pleased if you have twang: it gives him a good signal to work with! If you are doing work in the open air, twang is essential.

Twang is made in the larynx by tightening the aryepiglottic sphincter (AES for short). Let's see where this is:

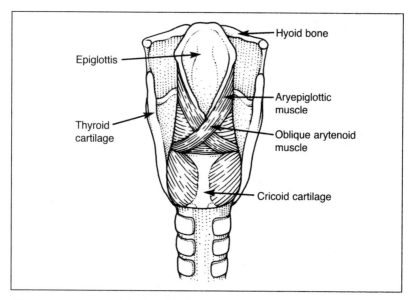

Diagram 1: the aryepiglottic sphincter

You can see that this ring of muscle is actually above the larynx and around the epiglottis. We need the epiglottis in swallowing. It lowers and closes up over the larynx to help protect the airways from foreign substances. When we tighten the AES – known colloquially as the twanger (a term coined by Helen Tiller in Australia) – the collar of the larynx narrows to one sixth of the vocal tract width, creating another resonator. Being narrower than the larynx, it resonates at a different frequency. This narrowing boosts the harmonics in the singer's formant.

We are now going to work at tightening the twanger. It is difficult to tighten one part of the larynx without tightening another, hence falling into constriction. For this reason there are a number of conditions you need to set up before attempting twang.

Exercise 1: PREPARATION FOR TWANG

You will need to review work from previous chapters at this stage. I will indicate which ones as we go through the preparation.

1. Raise your larynx by sirening silently up to the top of your range. Or, you can raise the larynx by performing the first part of a swallow. We did this in Chapter 3, page 23. Once you have raised the larynx, keep it high, and go though the Isolation Checklist so that there is no undue effort.
2. The back of the tongue must be high and in the ready position that you learned in Chapter 8, pages 103-5.
3. You must be retracted, so hold the silent laugh posture at the larynx.
4. You must be tilted in the thyroid as this enables you to sing with minimal effort in the vocal folds. Practise whining or miaowing to remind yourself of this tilted posture in the larynx.
5. Twang is accessed with the nasal port half-open. This enables you to fool the larynx out of completing the swallow manoeuvre. Practise talking with a half-open nasal port, checking that some of the sound is coming down your nose: 'EE'–'eh'–'AH'–'AW'–'OO' [iː]–[e]–[ɑː]–[ɔː]–[uː]. You learned how to access the half-open port in Chapter 6, page 59.

Having completed your preparation work, move on to the following exercise.

Exercise 2: ACCESSING TWANG

1. Make a cackling sound like a happy witch! What does feel like? The tongue will be high, and the mouth will be opening horizontally rather than vertically. You are probably cackling higher than your normal speaking pitch, and some of the sound will be coming down your nose. What does it sound like? Piercing and shrill as if coming from a small space.
2. Make the sound of one child taunting another in the playground: 'Nyea nyea-nyea nyea nyea'. The effort will be high up in the mouth and in the back of the tongue.

   Sing the pitches that go with this. Again, it's often easier to do it mid to high in your range. The 'n' part of the sound will be nasal because the port is open.

3. Make the sound of a quacking duck. Preferably a duck with attitude! Spread your mouth and make the space small inside, making sure that your tongue is up high at the back and touching the molars at the sides.

Students often report feeling as though they are singing from a smaller space when they use twang. This is absolutely accurate: the larynx is high, the tongue is high and you have made a smaller tube at the top of the larynx. So long as you are retracted this is OK. Now review what you have done before going to the next exercise.

Exercise 3: TWANGING

1. Prepare for twang by sirening up to a high note in your range. (Since you are sirening, you will be tilting the thyroid, and on a high note you will be raising the larynx.)
2. Stop the note and stay there, holding the posture of high larynx and tongue, and of tilting. Do not pull the jaw down.
3. Notice that you can breathe in and out through the nose in this position of the silent siren. Now check that you have retracted in the larynx by silently laughing.
4. Prepare to make the witch or the duck sounds. Move the soft palate a little way from the tongue as you cackle or quack.
5. Prepare to make the taunting child sounds. Scrape your tongue forwards along the hard palate as you move from 'nny' [ɲ] to 'y' [j] and into the vowel 'ae' [æ]. Remember that you are not singing yet; just make the noise and listen with your muscles.
   Notice the following as you do this exercise:
   i. The tongue is in ready position as for medialising the vowels;
   ii. You feel that you are 'singing from a smaller space';
   iii. You feel a greater push upwards of the tongue on the roof of the mouth as you pronounce 'ny' [ɲ] and a feeling in the nose as you start the sound. These sensations are the sense of effort associated with twanging;
   iv. The sound is different. Twang is actually quite unmistakable, and, in this instance, it is a difference in sound quality that you can hear for yourself. The sound should be bright and piercing!

SINGING WITH TWANG

Once you have got the feeling of twanging in a noise, you can start sustaining pitch. When you do this, try to pitch a note close to where you were making the noise; that way you will not lose the sensation of twanging. It is easy to 'drop out' of twang when we sing lower because the larynx is lowered for low pitches.

Some of the back vowels ('OO' [uː], 'aw' [ɒ], 'AW' [ɔː] and 'AH' [ɑː]) are difficult to twang. If you have mastered the higher tongue position for all the vowels as in medialisation, you should not have any trouble. Remember that for twang, the tongue needs to be high at all times. Keep the back of the tongue close and the sides spread so that you are maintain contact with the upper back molars.

Exercise 4: TWANGING WITH ALL VOWELS

1. Start by twanging on whatever vowel works best for you; it will be one of the front vowels: 'EE' [iː], 'eh' [e] or 'ae' [æ].
2. Now move from your first vowel through a sequence of five, singing 'nnyEE' to 'nnyOO' all on one note. Keep the mouth space small and the space in the larynx wide. Leave the back vowels 'AW' [ɔː] and 'OO' [uː] till last. Still round your lips on these last two.

'NYEE'   'NYeh'   'NYAH'   'NYAW'   'NYOO'

[ɲjiː]   [ɲje]   [ɲjɑː]   [ɲjɔː]   [ɲjuː]

3. Practise moving through the vowels quite fast using the sounds in 'miaow'. Put an 'n' at the front of the word instead of the 'm' and practise single notes this way.

'm – i – (e) – a – o – w'

'ny – i – (e) – a – o – w'

Watchpoints:

i. It is easy to 'scratch' at the larynx when learning to do twang; you must be retracted!

ii. Do not push for volume at the vocal folds. Even though twang sounds loud, you are not thickening the vocal fold muscle. Siren backwards down towards your starting note to get thinner vocal folds.

iii. Do not drive the breath. Do not push air through the twanger – it will make you constrict. Use no more air than you do for the siren.

iv. Your nasal port will still be half-open – this is OK.

v. Go through the rest of the Isolation Checklist to release unnecessary tensions in the body.

4. Now practise twanging your vowel sequence on every note of a descending scale. Notice what happens as you descend the scale: the larynx lowers and you lose your twang. To counteract this you must keep the larynx high. Do not make a 'bigger space' as you go down, but work to match the twang of your lower notes with the top notes.

It may be a surprise to hear that twang is made with thin folds. There is a reason for this: because of the narrowing at the top of the laryngeal tube, it is possible that some breath is pushed back down again over the vocal folds, causing them to stay closed for longer. This phenomenon is known as back-pressure. So, although you vocal folds are working no harder, the sound is loud when you are twanging, and it carries better. With twang, we get an increase in volume of 10–15 decibels. To give you an idea of what this means, a 3 decibel increase in volume represents a doubling of your sound!

Twang is not always nasal. You can do it with the nasal port closed as well. However, you must practise it initially with the port half-open. If the port is half-open it is easier to twang safely because the larynx will not be triggered into a swallow. Only when you have mastered nasal twang should you move on to oral twang.

Exercise 5: ORAL TWANG

1. Review opening and closing of the nasal port, page 58.
2. Make sure that when you close the port you do not move the tongue from its position against the upper back molars. Move only the soft palate.
3. Make sure that you do not lower the larynx when you close the port. Monitor its position with your fingers in the way I showed you in Exercises 3 and 4, Chapter 3, page 23.
4. Tighten the twanger as you sing very slowly: 'nnyEE' [ɲjiː]. Scrape your tongue along the hard palate as you sing the 'y' [j], and close the port as you sing 'EE'. (Remember that you close the port by raising the soft palate.)

   i. Do not drive the vocal folds at any point as you do this. The effort in the folds should be the same as in sirening, i.e. small!

   ii. If you lower your larynx or tongue as you go into oral twang, you will lose the twang. Keep the sides of the tongue on the upper back molars, sliding the body of the tongue forward as you close the port.

Song assignment: AMAZING GRACE

1. Siren the melody starting on a comfortable note in your range. Check that you are retracted and that the thyroid is tilted. The work in your vocal folds should be minimal so the sound is quiet.
2. Sing every note to either 'nnyae', 'nnyEE', or 'nneh', tightening the twanger as you do so. Use the initial 'n' to open the nasal port and press the tongue hard against the palate as you say the 'y' each time.

   Notice where you feel the effort when you do this:

   i. high up inside the mouth and at the back;

   ii. in the nose;

iii. not in the larynx. You should feel nothing in the larynx. If you do, you are putting the effort in the wrong place and that is not twang! Go back over the preparation exercises if you feel something at the larynx. You are either:

   a. Pressing too hard with the vocal folds (try going from an ordinary siren into the twanged note to compare your effort levels); or,

   b. trying to twang with a low larynx; it needs to be high; or,

   c. letting your tongue drop as you go from the 'n' into the vowel.

     When you twang, you need to give your vocal tract very clear messages!

3. Repeat stage 2, working through the Isolation Checklist. Note that:

   i. The effort level in the mouth will be high. Begin to isolate the jaw from this effort by chewing as you sing the notes. Sing the song as slowly as you need to – at whatever is your thinking speed.

   ii. You do not need much breath when you are twanging. Breathe when you need to. Notice what happens when you breathe in: you will probably make a silent gasp as you recoil into the breath. Make sure that you hold the effort in the mouth and nose, and stay retracted as you breathe in.

Check your posture as you walk around the room singing the song. You do not need to tense other muscles in the body because you are twanging.

4. Sing the words of the song, inserting a 'nny' [ɲj] before each vowel. Sing the vowels as written thus:

Remember that the back vowels are difficult to do when twanging.

Keep the tongue high and wide at all times as you do when medialising the vowels.

5. Repeat the song with the words as written, twanging throughout.
6. Repeat the song in other parts of your range.

There are risks associated with twanging. Many things we do with our voices can be risky if not properly executed and repeated over and again. There are two common problems with using twang that I have found in my teaching:

1. It is not good to add twang to a voice that has poor vocal fold approximation. In other words, if your vocal folds are not closing properly it is no good trying to add twang to get more volume. It will almost certainly lead to vocal problems. If your voice is always breathy and you think you may have this problem, seek the help of a good teacher before attempting twang.

2. If you are apt to drive at the folds (pressed phonation) you do not want to add to your vocal workload by twanging until you have learned to sing with thinner vocal folds. As a guideline, if you cannot siren well or sing softly with ease, it's not a good idea to twang until you have done some more work on your voice.

I mention these potential dangers because I have heard the results of actors who have heard about twang, caught on to it, and then abused their voices because they did not understand how to isolate the effort in the AES from other structures.

Occasionally I have worked with singers who have too much twang. Usually the twang is part of their habitual speech pattern, and it feels normal to twang in singing as well. The musical director of one of my students complained that 'her vowels weren't true enough and that her sound was too wide'. I showed her how to make the vocal tract longer and how to get rid of the twang so that she could choose to use it or not. We also worked at making the twang a little warmer by rounding the front of the mouth. If you want to switch your twanger off, lower the larynx.

Once you have got the hang of your twanger, you will find it invaluable as part of your sound palette. Record yourself singing *Amazing Grace* with and without twang, and you'll hear what I mean. You will find that you can use twang to add excitement to a note, to make a crescendo, to add brightness to notes that are dull in your voice, and you can use it as a voice quality. Twang changes the shape of your instrument and creates an identifiable voice quality. The change in tonal colour is rather like going from a clarinet to a trumpet: you no longer have only one sound! More of this in Chapter 12.

SECTION 3
Working the text

This section represents the culmination of the work you have done so far. Getting to the act of performance (what I have called the act of singing) is what it's all about. Professional actors will quite often comment that they find it much more difficult to get connected with a song than straight text. What follows in this section is a process that will enable you to put together your integrity as an actor with the demands of the music.

Chapter 10 guides you step-by-step through applying all the techniques you have learned so far. If you were a novice singer at the beginning of the book, you should use this process the first few times you learn a song. If you are more experienced, read the chapter through and use it as a checklist for song preparation. Chapter 10 can also serve as an index for vocal trouble-shooting when you are learning new material. Chapter 11 is about making sure the audience can understand what you are saying. There is no point in singing the song unless they can hear the words – you might as well be singing for yourself!

The final two chapters are about making choices – choices about voice quality and acting. This is where your imagination and creativity come into play. These two chapters represent only part of a process that you will repeat many times with many variations. In teaching this part of the work, I have learned as much from my students as they from me. At this point in performance preparation I become a facilitator, working with the actor to find his or her way through the material in the way that is most truthful for them.

In order to be truly confident with the song, you must be on top of it musically, dramatically, knowing what you want and how you're going to get it, and what you are going to do with it – otherwise, do not bother. Do the work so that you can play your intentions 100%; then it will not feel like work. The next four chapters will, I hope, give you a process for achieving just that.

Chapter 10

Putting it together

The aim of this chapter is to show you how to apply the techniques you have learned so far. After all, this is what technique is for. In practising the exercises given the last nine chapters you have been building your instrument. Because we have done this step by step, you will understand what you are doing with your voice and will be able to put the work into practice quickly.

Learning a song is not just about memorising the melody and the words. By now you will realise that the 'learning' involves 'instrument-playing', muscular control and co-ordination. As we build in the things you have learned, I will show you how to target some of the vocal and musical difficulties that arise in song-learning.

To begin, you need a strategy for learning the music; what follows is a pretty near foolproof method for learning a song. You will need a short song of your own choice.

Song assignment: YOUR SONG

1. Working with the words
Start with the text only; do not bother with the melody. Read the text aloud in ordinary speech, paying attention to stress, inflection and meaning. Some of these will change slightly when you add the melody and rhythm, but that doesn't matter at this stage.

2. Adding the rhythm
1. You will need some help with this stage if you cannot read music. Work with a good song coach or a friend (an honest friend!), or as a last choice, with a good recording of the song. In general, when you are learning a new song, do not choose a jazz or cover version; these will be different from the original, and you will waste valuable time learning a version that is intended for a different kind of performance.

2. Say the words line by line in the rhythm of the music. You will find that you are intoning the words as you sustain each syllable for its note value. Do not cheat on this bit; notice how the emphasis of certain syllables and even whole words may alter from your first reading. This is a good time to:

i. scan the phrase lengths and pay attention to airflow;

ii. notice difficult sounds.

I find this stage of the song-learning is critical: many actors have difficulty with singing because they cannot get used to having both the rhythm and pace of the text dictated by the music. Think of the musical structure as an extra dimension that you can use in performance, rather than as a straightjacket. More of this later. Do not move on to the next stage until you are confident that you have mastered the note rhythms.

3. Sirening and mirening

1. Siren the melody. Sirening is a wonderful way of programming in the melodic line when learning a song. It will set your voice up for singing rather than speaking. It will also enable you to direct your attention towards difficult intervals between notes, and to recognise any notes that are in an awkward part of your range.

When you siren:

i. remember to do so quietly so that you can 'listen with the muscles';

ii. pay attention to the larynx and check that you are retracted;

iii. pay attention to the larger muscles in the vocal tract. Do you need to be anchored to get any of the notes? Do you need to raise or lower the larynx?

2. Miren the melody. (You can revise mirening from Chapter 6, page 64.) Siren 'ng' [ŋ] at the back of your mouth and mouth the words of the song at the front of your mouth. This is great for co-ordinating the muscles of articulation.

If you have worked through these stages carefully, you will have made a mental and physical template for memorising the song correctly. It's so easy to miss out one part of this process by trying to learn the song in one go, and it only leads to difficulties at a later stage.

4. Targeting constriction

Sing the song with the words, melody and rhythm. Then, target the difficulties. Good practice is all about awareness. Notice what you find easy and do well, and what you find difficult. Identifying and targeting your difficulties is the main reason for practising. Why would you need to practise what you already do well? To give you an idea of what I mean, I shall now give you a number of instances in music that might lead to laryngeal constriction:

1. Problem notes in your range

From the work we did in Chapter 5, you already have a good idea of where you have problem notes. If you find these notes are giving you trouble in the context of the song, siren the problem phrase slowly and remember to retract in the larynx when you go into the vowels. You may find it helpful to sing the notes on 'EE' [iː] first, and to scroll through to the correct vowel. Anchoring the neck will also help you here.

2. Sudden leaps

Large intervals, (e.g. the interval of a 7th in Sondheim's *'Anyone Can Whistle'*) can trigger constriction.

The solution is to prepare for the pitch *before* you actually sing it. You can do this by silently sirening up to your target note (or down, for the downward leap) from the note before. This way, your larynx has all the messages it needs to make the note. Do this at thinking speed first, then gradually increase until you can do it in time with the music.

3. Breathing in

An in-breath can often be a trigger for constriction, particularly in the middle or at the ends of phrases. In both instances you should stop singing and hold the sensation of silently laughing at the larynx *before* you take the breath. Then continue with the next word or phrase. Once you have practised this a few times, your muscles will remember to hold the silent laugh posture at the larynx when you breathe in, even at performance speed.

4. Voiceless stops

These are the sounds 'p', 't', 'k', 's' and 'ch' [tʃ]. You cannot sing an unvoiced consonant, even if it is in the middle of a word. The breath stream is stopped before in order to make these consonants, and the vocal

folds will be apart. To see what I mean, experiment with the first word of Gershwin's *'Summertime'*.

Notice that you cannot pitch on the 't' itself, nor, indeed, on the 's' at the beginning of the word. (The 's' is a voiceless fricative.)

i. Check that you are making the consonant with the right muscles (see Chapter 11, pages 149-50);

ii. Check that you are not voicing, and that there is no constriction;

iii. Silently siren to the note you are about to sing, so that the pitch is prepared.

5. Problems with breath

In Chapter 4, I outlined three aspects of breathing which might cause problems: not allowing the breath to come in, insufficient airflow, and over-breathing. Let's consider these in more detail, one at a time

1. The in-breath

Use the elastic recoil every time you need or want to breathe in: at the ends of phrases, to make a dramatic point mid-phrase, or when you have ended a word with a stopped consonant. Each time you need to breathe in, release the abdominal wall at the navel. It is a useful to practise this slowly and then wait a second while you check that you are retracted. The body tends to relax as we breathe in, so it can be easy to constrict when singing recommences.

(Remember that you do not need to use up all your air each time you sing a phrase. Whenever you want to breathe, let go of the abdominal wall and recoil into the new breath.)

2. Monitoring airflow

Examine your airflow; is it sufficient to the task? If your airflow is insufficient, the sound will be 'pressed' or 'driven' when you sing. It may be quite loud, but you will tire easily because you are making the vocal folds work too hard. If this is the case, do the following:

i. Practise the song, phrase by phrase, on a rolled 'R' or lip trill, checking that the navel is going towards the backbone as you sing.

ii. Then repeat the song using the words, but starting each phrase with the rolled 'R' or lip trill to check the airflow.

3a. Breathy tone

If the sound is breathy (and you don't want it to be), this is a sign that you are not creating enough resistance in the vocal folds. In this case the solution is to increase your vocal fold mass, reduce your airflow and anchor the body. (Review the work we did in Chapter 7, pages 68-9, on levels of work in the vocal folds, and fold mass.)

i. Take a phrase from the song that you feel is breathy and under-powered. Start the first note with a glottal onset, using first 'EE' [iː] and then the vowel that is given. Pay attention to the effort level you feel in the vocal folds, and maintain it throughout the rest of the phrase as you bring in the words again. This will help to give you better closure of the vocal folds.

ii. Now sing the phrase silently, applying the anchoring exercises from Chapter 7, pages 70-3. Pay attention to the effort you are making to anchor, rather than to the breath.

iii. Sing the phrase again, with the increased effort in the vocal folds and in the body. Notice that you are now breathing out less! This strategy should address breathy tone.

You should also check what is happening as you onset the tone at the beginning of phrases. Are you pushing air as you start the sound? You do not need to do this; you will find it more breath efficient to use a glottal or simultaneous onset.

3b. Over-breathing: not allowing the vocal folds to control the outflow of air

Overbreathing is a common problem not always recognised for what it is. In this instance, the vocal folds are closing properly, but the student is so fixated on 'breath' that he or she does not allow the vocal folds to control the outflow of air. Good breath use is a matter of resistance and flow (Chapter 4, pages 31-2). If you are pushing air up against vocal folds that are already closing, you are asking them to work harder and harder. Generally, you will develop a wobble if you are doing this, as the whole larynx starts to shake as it joins in the fight to resist the breath! You will also feel that you are working too hard: something in the effort equation is out of balance. The solution to this problem is very similar to the one above.

i.   Begin by *reducing* your airflow.

ii.   Retract in the larynx. (Constriction creeps in when we are overworking the breath.)

iii.   Anchor the torso. (This will help to hold the breath back.)

6. Breathing to the task

This is a complex issue and I could easily write a whole chapter on it! You may have noticed that the last two problems were actually fixed with strategies you learned in Chapter 7. Many 'breathing' problems are not actually anything to do with the breath: they are effort issues and can be solved by adjusting what is happening in the larynx and the body. As a practice exercise, let us suppose that you have chosen to work on a sustained ballad, such as *'I've Never Been in Love Before'* by Frank Loesser from *Guys and Dolls*. You will want to sing the whole of the first phrase in one breath, with a full and lyrical tone.

Assuming that you are lacking sustaining power, now is the time to engage the muscles in the waistband.

i. Sing the first phrase on the rolled 'R' or lip trill. Put your hands around the waistband (see Chapter 4, pages 37-8) so that you can feel its lateral movement.

ii. When you want to breathe in, release the waistband. You should re-engage it as you start to sing the next phrase on the rolled 'R' or lip trill. If you are performing the elastic recoil correctly and engaging the waistband, you will quickly build enough sustaining power to sing each of the first four phrases, one after the other. (Breathe in after the words 'before', 'safe', and 'score'.)

iii. Some Musical Directors will ask you to sing the following phrase in one breath. You may find this a challenge.

But   this   is   wine   that's   all   too   strange   and   strong

Continue working with the rolled 'R' or lip trill. As you sing the note for the word 'wine', which is three beats long (three-quarter note), consciously engage the waistband on the long note, and you will make it to the end of the phrase.

iv. Now add the words. Notice that the airflow is different because you have introduced consonants (see Chapter 4, page 33). You will be aware of this, particularly with the fricatives and stops. The fricatives will use up a lot of air when you make them, so you will feel more work in the abdominal wall; the airflow will be held for stopped consonants, and then released. You will find that you can easily breathe in again if you have a voiceless stop at the end of a word, e.g. after 'that's'.

v. You'll remember from Chapter 4, page 31 that I talked about different levels of resistance and flow according to the voice quality you have chosen at any point in your song. Your dynamic level will also have an effect on your breath use. You will have a better understanding of how this works once you have done the work on voice qualities in Chapter 12. For now, I just want to remind you of the points I made about effort levels in the vocal folds and the effect this has on the breath. Your sense of work in the support muscles will vary according to the task in hand:

a. Pay attention to the level of resistance in the vocal folds. How hard are the folds working to resist the breath?

b. Do not push air as you start the tone unless you are singing a consonant that demands this.

c. If you have to breathe in fast, always maintain your effort to retract in the larynx.

7. Adding the anchoring

We are now applying the work learned in Chapter 7 on dynamic control. You do not necessarily need to be anchored all the time; it really depends on the task in hand. Nor do you need to be anchored at the same level throughout a song; you will be adjusting all the time to suit your needs and the needs of the music. However, if you want a focused and 'resonant' tone, you will need a degree of vocal tract anchoring (head, neck and face) most of the time.

i. Sing your song phrase by phrase. Elongate the first note of each phrase, and, as you do so, sing the elongated note first relaxed, and then anchored. You will feel a difference in your effort levels and the sound will be 'bigger'. Continue with the rest of the phrase, holding the effort of anchoring throughout. Make sure you are retracted when you do this, and that you remember to recoil when you breathe in.

ii. Apply the same principles in anchoring the torso. Remember that if you have a big voice, you will benefit from a degree of torso anchoring all the time. Otherwise, use it as you need it. Once you have rehearsed the song a few times, applying these techniques, you will find that the anchoring muscles come into play more automatically.

8. Checking the nasal port

You are now applying the work learned in Chapter 6. It's very simple; unless you have chosen to use a nasal voice quality, or are singing in an accent that requires a lot of nasality, there are two rules:

i. Your nasal port should be closed on all the vowels;

ii. Your nasal port should be closed on all consonants except the sounds 'n', 'ng' [ŋ] and 'm'.

Check for this by doing the nose test. Sing each phrase of the song, extracting the vowels only. Hold your nose to check that the nasal port is closed.

As a practice example, here's the opening of *'Autumn'* by Maltby and Shire, from *Starting Here, Starting Now*:

Au - tumn___

Make sure you open your nasal port fully and sound the 'm' very strongly because nasal consonants are not easily heard. When you continue with 'it feels like' you must make sure to close the nasal port again.

In your own song, underline the nasal consonants in the words. Practise each of these words on a single note, checking that you first open and then close the nasal port.

9. Medialising the vowels

As you go through your song, you'll notice that it's more difficult to make a good sound on some words than others. You will need to apply the work from Chapter 8. (See Chapter 8, pages 103-7). Remember that not all vowels are equal, and that you may need to medialise.

i. Begin by getting the tongue into the 'ready' position: the back is high and spread so that you can touch the upper back molars. The tip of the tongue is touching the bottom front teeth.

ii. Sing each word that you find difficult on 'EE' [iː] to begin with, then 'scroll through' the vowels until you reach the correct one for the word you are singing. Keep some contact between the sides of the tongue at the back and the upper back molars at all times.

iii. When you have reached your target vowel, hold it, and check that you are not clamping the jaw. Make sure that you are retracted.

iv. Sing the word again with the same tongue placement, going straight into the vowel as written and at normal speed.

Here's another example from Maltby and Shire's 'Autumn':

re - call

This is from the bridge section. The music becomes more intense and the melody rises. The highest note in the song (E flat) is on the vowel 'AW' [ɔː] (or [ɒː] in Standard U.S) for which your tongue is at its lowest in normal speech. You will want to medialise to avoid singing a high note with a flat tongue! Use the 'EE' on the first syllable of the word to check that your tongue is in 'ready' position, and sing the top note to 'EE' before attempting it on 'AW'. Maintain a close tongue with the sides on the molars.

10. Using twang to match resonance

Sometimes, when you are singing a phrase at the bottom of your range, the note disappears. The voice is not a perfect instrument, and some notes will sound better in your voice than others. In this case, use twang; it will enable the listeners to hear the note without you straining your voice. To add twang to your sound remember that there are certain requirements:

i. You must be retracted in the larynx and your tongue must be high, wide and flat;

ii. The larynx must be high.

1. Prepare for twanging by tilting the thyroid (the miaow or whine sensation).

2. Take the note or notes from your song that require more volume, and

sing them first on 'nnyEE' [ɲjiː] or 'nnyae' [ɲjæ], keeping the twanger tightened.

3. Repeat the notes, holding on to them for a little longer, so that you have time to check your nasal port. Pinch your nose after going into the vowel to check that you have closed the port. (If you want nasal twang, you can leave out this stage.)

4. Now sing the correct vowels inserting 'nny' [ɲj] at the beginning of each note. Check the nasal port again if necessary.

5. Finally, keeping your twanger tightened, sing the words.

Work with twang on either of the following song assignments.

Song assignment 1: THE OPENING PHRASE OF 'WITH EVERY BREATH I TAKE' BY CY COLEMAN AND DAVID ZIPPEL.

Sing the opening phrase, 'There's not a morning that I open up my eyes'. The back vowel 'morning' is sung on a low note. This is double trouble!
i. Sing, 'There's not a 'nnyEE'-'nnyEE' that I open ...'
ii. Then sing, 'There's not a 'nyor-nyi-ng' that I open ...'
iii. Finally, sing the words as written, keeping the twanger on. You will almost certainly get a better bottom note.

Song assignment 2: THE BRIDGE PASSAGE OF 'EMPTY CHAIRS AT EMPTY TABLES' BY SCHÖNBERG AND BOUBLIL.

Work on the phrase 'From the table in the corner'. This is usually sung by a tenor, who needs to make a crescendo on a phrase containing low A, often the bottom note in his range.
i. Do not lower the larynx at this point; it will only make your voice quieter and you will not be able to make the crescendo needed to indicate the rising excitement in this passage. Raise the larynx before you even start the phrase. (You are now applying work from Chapter 3.)
ii. Tighten the twanger.
iii. Sing 'nyom-nye nyable nyin', and so on up to 'corner', keeping the back of the tongue high. You will find that the notes speak better. If you add some anchoring as the phrase continues you will be able to make a good crescendo without straining.

11. Raising and lowering the larynx

In Chapter 3, when we were doing laryngeal orienteering, you learned how to raise and lower the larynx. In very general terms, you will want to raise the larynx for singing the top end of your range and to lower it at the bottom end. In addition, once you have got the larynx to a place where you can make the pitch most easily, you have the option to alter your tonal quality by raising or lowering. Lowering the larynx will deepen the tone, and raising the larynx will make it brighter (you are changing the length of your resonating tube when you do this).

1. Lowering the larynx

Perhaps, if you are dance trained, or have an habitual speech pattern that is high larynx, you feel that your tone is too shrill. I would like to stress that this is purely a matter of taste and not to do with vocal health; a low larynx is not necessarily a healthy one! In addition, you may have difficulty reaching the bottom notes of your song.

i. Using the yawn-sigh manoeuvre from Chapter 3, page 23, lower your larynx.

ii. Now take this a stage further by breathing out as if sobbing deeply. Do it for a few moments, keeping the larynx low, even on the in-breath.

iii. Take the passage of your song that you would like to work, and sing it with the larynx in this low posture. Notice that it takes considerable effort to hold the larynx in this low position. Your tone will be deeper and darker in quality.

2. Raising the larynx

Perhaps you have had a classically-based singing training and wish to sing a pop song. Alternatively, you may have been told that your singing voice is too 'dark and covered'. It may be simply that you cannot get a high note in your song that you know is in your range.

i. Silently siren to the top of your range and hold the larynx in this position. Make sure you are retracting the false vocal folds. Or, start to swallow and stop at the point of raising the larynx. Again, hold the position and retract the false vocal folds. (See Chapter 3, page 23.)

ii. Sing the note or notes that you are working on with the larynx in this high posture. It may well feel as though you are singing from a smaller space (which you are), but you will find the top notes are accessed more easily this way. Remember that it is the smaller musical instruments that are higher in range. Your own vocal instrument is immensely flexible and can change length.

If you sing a whole phrase or song with a high larynx it may sound shrill to your ears. This may not be the case in the ears of the listener, and high larynx production will carry well because of the way the ear hears.

Remember that raising and lowering the larynx is a matter of degree; there is also a neutral position that is somewhere in-between. It is not necessary, nor desirable, to fix the larynx in any one position. It needs to be able to move up or down for easy access to the pitches first, and then manoeuvred to adjust vocal quality. I will talk more about changes in voice quality in Chapter 12.

Practice and rehearsal

You have now completed an eleven-point plan for working a song. You may be wondering how long your practice time needs be if you are to do all this. Let's consider warm-up time first. I discussed this in the introduction to Section 2 and mentioned the importance of being physically and mentally prepared for work. Warm-up time can be brief; if you can get your siren working, you are ready to practise. Some people need to remind themselves about retraction and anchoring in order to 'get their voice going'. Both these techniques can be rehearsed silently.

If you are learning new skills, twenty minutes is a good time span for your practice; this is considered to be our optimum time for intense concentration. When you are learning and memorising large chunks of music, you do not need to sing aloud all the time. You will use your time and voice more efficiently if you learn your music using the siren and miren; it also disturbs the neighbours less!

When you are involved long technical rehearsals, or rehearsing during a run of a show, it may be desirable to 'mark' with your voice. Many people do not know how to do this properly and either tire themselves by singing full out, or de-voice in the wrong way. Here's how to mark:

i. Set your effort level in the vocal folds by the siren; your vocal folds are working minimally in this mode.

ii. Mouth the words as you do in mirening and then close the nasal port as you go into the words. (Remember that the port is still open for the nasal consonants.)

iii. You will now be singing with thin folds. The sound will be quiet but clear.

So there it is: the nuts and bolts of learning a song in one chapter! You have only been able to achieve this because of the work covered in the previous chapters. First comes the understanding of the vocal instrument, next the organisation of different structures and muscles groups, then the singing. All the way through it is important to monitor your effort, because singing is a complex act that requires muscles to work together. If something in your effort equation is out of balance, you will either experience discomfort or the sound will not be what you want. Once you have your vocal mechanism organised and have set your effort levels appropriately, you will find that you can begin to forget how you do the singing and concentrate on *what* you are singing.

Chapter 11

Am I communicating?

Originally I was going to call this chapter 'Can you hear me?' because I wanted to talk about diction. Diction is a rather old fashioned word reminiscent of elocution lessons and speaking nicely! So what is good diction? Good diction means that you will be understood, not just heard. You have learned enough already in the course of this book to make yourself heard, but can the audience understand what you are saying? Good diction is a large part of something fundamental to the actor: the need to communicate.

Your need is to communicate: Your psychological state, the message of the song, and what is happening in the story at the time of your singing. No matter how hard you are working as an actor, no matter how accomplished your timing and technique, if the audience cannot understand the words of your song as you are singing them, they will be losing something of your message. Even if they can work out what you were saying in hindsight, you will have lost them for those few precious seconds. So diction is a key issue.

Singing is characterised by sustained pitch; this is the fundamental difference between speech and song. Pitch and the melodic line are carried largely by the vowels. Consonants, particularly stopped consonants, interrupt the melodic line. At a very simple level, for example, you cannot sing on 't', only on the vowel that follows it. Even when we sing voiced consonants, there is some interruption or filtering of sound by the work done to make the consonant, so we are not able to hear the pitch as clearly as on vowels. Because of their nature, consonants are harder to hear than the vowels, so they are double trouble to a singer: they don't carry the line and they don't carry well to the ear. No wonder it is difficult to hear singers' words! Please don't think that the sound man can save you here; he will only amplify what you already do. The relationship of vowel to consonant remains the same even when you are miked.

VOCAL LINE (SINGER-ORIENTATED DICTION)

Using vocal line is the traditional way of dealing with the problem of consonants. I want you to explore this concept through the following exercise:

Exercise 1: VOCAL LINE

1. Sing through the melody of the song you worked on for Chapter 10. Sing it line by line to a rolled 'R' or to a lip trill. Producing a vocal line means keeping the breath going between each note in the phrase – not stopping between notes (unless there's a rest written in) – and keeping the both the airflow and breath-pressure constant.

2. Sing the song with the vowels only, so that the line is unbroken in each phrase. When you have a syllable containing a diphthong, hold the first part of the sound almost until the end of the note so that you make a very even sound throughout.

3. Sing the song with the words. Sustain all the note values as written, using the vowels. Do the consonants quickly, taking away as little time as possible from the sung vowels. Keep the dynamics constant within each sung note, paying attention particularly to longer note values. Look at the extract below from *'Anyone Can Whistle'* by Sondheim to see how this could be written out. Notice how the consonants at the end of each word or syllable have been put onto the next note in order to keep the line as uninterrupted as possible.

That is what we mean by vocal line: it will enable you to be heard, to make a good sound, and for the audience to hear only a string of well-sung vowels! It's a solution that focuses on the melodic line and beauty of the voice as communicators of the song's message. Unfortunately the audience have little chance of hearing the words with any clarity because this solution does not address the acoustic imbalance between the vowels and the consonants. It also means that, because they cannot hear the words properly, the audience start to concentrate on how good or bad your voice is or how well you are singing, rather than listening to the message of the song and so being engaged in the creative process. You had better have a good voice if you are singing like this because your voice is all they'll hear. This solution to the diction dichotomy is inappropriate for theatre singing.

Listener-Orientated Diction

The alternative solution is to make your diction listener-orientated instead of singer-orientated. Since the vowels are louder that the consonants, especially when we are singing, the solution must be to enlarge the consonants in some way.

The law of temporal summation (one of the precepts of acoustics) states that, 'If an acoustic event is shorter than 250 milliseconds, it must be higher in amplitude to reach the threshold of hearing' (Zwislocki, J. *Theory of Temporal Auditory Summation* Acoustic Society, America Vol 32 1960). Normally consonants are shorter than this time span, and the vowels, of course, are longer. In order to lift the consonants to the threshold of hearing (+250ms), we either have to make them louder or longer. Otherwise, they cannot compete with the vowels in the hearing stakes!

But consonants are not the only problem with diction, or intelligibility in singing; they are one of a number. We are now going to explore the five key issues relating to diction. I shall present a practice problem (or problems) with each of them.

Targets for making yourself understood.

1. Sing authentic vowels. You are singing in English or American in the vast majority of musical theatre repertoire, so do not use Italian vowels.

2. Sing *all* the sounds in compound vowels.

3. Work the consonants. Understand how they are made and exaggerate the perceptual cues for the audience.

4. Do not run words into each other, making nonsense words.

5. Do not distort words and syllables, even if the composer does.

1. Authentic vowels

Sing authentic vowels. Sing the vowels that are idiomatic to the language, not Italianate vowels. This seems so obvious that I think we sometimes forget it. You will be far more intelligible if you sing the same vowels as for speech. Many singers do not do this because of a more traditional training, and for modern musical theatre it is unacceptable. You will commonly find in books about singing that the vowels used in singing are: 'AH', 'ehh', 'EE', 'ohh', 'OO'. These Italian vowels are still used as a basis for singing training by some teachers, with the other vowel sounds taught as modifications of these five. If you have studied phonetics, and fortunately many actors do so now as part of their training, you will know that some of these sounds are not even used in English and that we have many more besides. In addition, a great deal of musical theatre literature needs to be sung in Standard American.

Rather than using Italian vowels to modify English vowels in singing, you should use medialisation. This will enable you to sing any vowel, long or short, with clarity and without altering the colour of the language. The lengthening of our short vowel sounds in English are a case in point.

Problem 1: elongation of short vowels

In Stephen Sondheim's *'I Remember'*, the words 'ink' and 'think' appear near the end of the song, both on four-beat notes. In English (and American) the vowel is 'ih' [ɪ] (exactly as we'd say 'ink') and not 'EE' [iː]. The problem here is that 'ih' is a short vowel, set to a long note. It would be all too easy to turn the sound into the longer 'EE'. The solution is to work with all the sounds in the words, using the nasal consonants, and going toward the closure indicated by the final 'k' in each word. So here is an instance where you can get good effect by gradually opening your nasal port on a vowel. In this way, you can keep the listener interested in the long note as you change resonance on it, without sacrificing the text.

Problem 2: the neutrals

The so-called neutral vowels 'uh' [ə] and 'UH' [ʌ] are often dubbed non-singing vowels. This is unfortunate when they are a major feature of English languages. If you change these vowels into something else when singing, you will be making an aesthetic choice in favour of the beauty of your own voice. If you want to put the audience first, you should sing the written vowels and use medialisation to help shape your sound to the ear of the listener. If you want an example, just think of how often you have to sing the word love. Which vowel do you sing when this word is on a long note? Many people sing 'lAHv' [lɑːv] or 'lawv' [lɒv]. Try singing the right vowel next time and see if you get a better effect!

Problem 3: singing close vowels on high notes

Some singers experience difficulty singing high notes on the close vowels 'EE' [iː] and 'OO' [uː]. If you have been trained to make a bigger space for the high notes, it will feel wrong to sing these vowels correctly. Many singers actually write 'AH' over any note above the stave. If you do this, you are not being listener orientated. An extreme example might be the ending of *'A Call from the Vatican'* (*Nine*, Maury Yestern) which is sung on high C, and *'Music of the Night'* (*Phantom of the Opera*, Andrew Lloyd Webber) which is sung on high G sharp.

Gui - do

be

If you change the vowels to access these notes more easily, you are making an aesthetic choice. It's perfectly possible to sing the notes on the written vowels; you just may not like the sound you hear! Here's how to work at this problem:

1. Make sure you can access the note comfortably on a siren.

2. Quietly (i.e. at siren volume) move from the 'ng' [ŋ] into the written vowel.

In the case of *'Call from the Vatican'*, I would voice the 'g' on pitch before singing the 'OO' [uː] and 'EE' [iː], because that is the first sound in the word. Don't try to do it too loud – top C is already loud. Don't' worry if the sound isn't beautiful – it's written as a scream!

In *'Music of the Night'*, notice how little effort there is in the larynx as you do the 'ng' [ŋ] siren; that is about the right amount of effort needed when you voice the 'b' for the word. When go back to the words, make sure you actually sing the 'b' on the written pitch, not below. You will find it much easier to sing the 'EE' properly if you do this.

3. In both instances, use anchoring to stabilise the note if you want to increase your volume from the siren.

2. Compound vowels

You should sing all the sounds in compound vowels. In Chapter 8, under the heading 'Vowel Formation', we looked at the British and American simple vowels or monophthongs. At this point in the book I wanted you to focus on getting your voice set up and to tune your vocal tract resonance. Now is the time to analyse more complex vowel sounds, and to understand how to sing them so that they are intelligible to the audience. I mentioned above that a lot of traditional singing training focuses on 'pure' vowel sounds that actually are not a main feature of either British or American speech. When I was training as a singer, we were told that English is the hardest language for singing because it is full of diphthongs, and that they do not project well. This is nonsense; you just have to know how to manage the compound vowels. When I finally learned phonetics, I saw that it is possible to do this. There is a tradition in British Choral singing that diphthongs should be avoided; this is because it is difficult to control a whole body of people changing vowel mid-note. When you are singing solo, it doesn't make sense for you to minimise the diphthongs and triphthongs; you will distort the words and the audience won't be able to hear them.

Overleaf there is a list of the Standard British and American compound vowels. Take some time going through the list speaking the words aloud, feeling the transition as you move from one vowel to another. Note that there are a number of triphthongs to deal with; they often read as two syllables, but actually contain three vowels and two transitions. Take time as you say these sounds.

Standard British Vowels: Diphthongs

Centring   [ɪə]   as in n**ear**, f**ear**, **rear**

             [eə]   as in th**ere**, h**air**, f**air**

             [ʊə]   as in mat**ure**, p**oor**, l**ure**

Closing   [eɪ]   as in th**ey**, s**ay**, aw**ay**

             [aɪ]   as in t**i**me, h**i**gh, awr**y**

             [ɔɪ]   as in b**oy**, l**oi**n, andr**oi**d

             [əʊ]   as in n**o**, s**ew**, ag**o**

             [aʊ]   as in h**ow**, l**ou**d, v**ow**

Standard British Vowels: Triphthongs

             [eɪə]   as in pl**ayer**, conv**eyor**, sl**ayer**

             [aɪə]   as in sc**ience**, v**iolet**, f**ire**

             [ɔɪə]   as in l**awyer**, r**oyal**, t**oil**

             [əʊə]   as in l**ower**, m**ower**, bl**ower**

             [aʊə]   as in p**ower**, s**our**, fl**ower**

Standard American Vowels: Diphthongs

Centring   [ɪɚ]   as in r**ear**, n**ear**, app**ear**

             ɛɚ]   as in th**ere**, h**air**, f**air**

             [ɑɚ]   as in c**ar**, s**ar**dine, t**ar**

             [ɔɚ]   as in m**ore**, **Or**pheus, p**ore**

             [ʊɚ]   as in p**ure**, end**ure**, cont**our**

Closing   [eɪ]   as in th**ey**, s**ay**, aw**ay**

             [aɪ]   as in t**i**me, h**i**gh, awr**y**

             [ɔɪ]   as in b**oy**, l**oi**n, andr**oi**d

             [oʊ]   as in **o**ver, ag**o**, v**o**gue

             [aʊ]   as in h**ow**, all**ow**, v**ow**

Standard American Vowels: Triphthongs

             [eɪɚ]   as in pl**ayer**, conv**eyor**, sl**ayer**

             [aɪɚ]   as in d**ire**, adm**ire**, f**ire**

             [ɔɪɚ]   as in l**awyer**, f**oyer**, empl**oyer**

             [oʊɚ]   as in l**ower**, m**ower**, bl**ower**

             [aʊɚ]   as in p**ower**, s**our**, fl**ower**

Problem 1: diphthongs

Look again at *'I Remember'* (Sondheim). You will find a lot of notes set to compound vowels: 'light and noise and bees and boys and days.'

Let's consider 'light' and 'days', as their note values are different. The tempo is slow, so you can afford to divide 'light' into three quaver beats. As a general rule, the time ratio for how long to spend on the first and second sounds of a diphthong is two-to-one. In the case of 'light', this means singing 'a' [ɑː] for two quavers and 'ih' [ɪ] for one. (If your note is not easily divisible by three, think of the first vowel in the diphthong as being twice as long.) So it would look like this on manuscript:

light   [la _____ ɪt]

What about 'days' which is sung on a seven beat note? You could spend four beats on 'eh' [e], two on 'ih' [ɪ], and one beat for the final 'z' [z], but I think that this is still not making the consonant long enough to be easily heard. So you might start to move from the 'eh' to the 'ih' earlier – say around the fourth beat – and so give more time to the 'z'. (There again, you might want to make the consonant longer in a different theatre acoustic, and we haven't allowed any time yet for the 'd'!)

So you begin to see the problem: the audience needs to hear all the sounds in the word, and you have to make decisions about how you are going to parcel out the vowels within the given note value. Make sure you use all your vowel targets.

Problem 2: triphthongs

You'll see that all the British triphthongs end with the schwa 'uh' [ə] , which becomes the rhotic 'urr' [ɚ] in American. I suggest, as a practice exercise, that you just sing them on one note, feeling the transitions your tongue has to make in order to get through all the sounds. Not everyone agrees as to how triphthongs should be managed, even in speech, because there are so many variations in their pronunciation. In music, you will often find these sound set to two notes as in the example below from Maltby and Shire's *'Closer Than Ever'*.

fi - re   [fa   ɪ   ə]
              [fa   ɪ   ɚ] (U.S)

In this case you should sing the first two vowels on the first note, as shown, singing the final vowel on the second note. Continue to medialise as you make this transition. Occasionally you will have a word with a triphthong set to one note. Sometimes the composer will put in an apostrophe in order to indicate to you that you should cut the vowels down to two – as in this case from the *Beggar's Opera* – but they don't always bother. You must use your judgement in this case – how many of the sound targets do you need to make in order to be intelligible to the audience? Get someone who doesn't know your song to listen to you singing and tell you if they can understand the problem.

In some styles of music, the relative space given to each vowel will change. It's acceptable in pop music to move on earlier to the second vowel in the syllable and to hold it for longer than the first.

Problem 3: the glides r [r], *w* [w], *y* [j]
These sounds are known as approximants because there is no true point of obstruction. They used to be called semi-vowels because they behave like vowels, and, in English, they often substitute as spelling for a vowel (e.g. 'beauty', 'vow', 'near'). (In some period music you might tap or roll the 'R' in the middle or beginning of a word, in which case it would not be classed as an approximant.) In singing you should treat these sounds as you do compound vowels. Sing all the transitions that are present in the sounds, and sing them on the pitch of the note.

1. Sing the word 'world' slowly. What is the first sound you make as you say the 'w'? It's 'OO' [uː]. There are two key points here:

a. You need to pitch the 'OO' on the note you are singing, not somewhere else. (People often pitch it below the written note.)

b. You will need to move off the 'OO' straightaway because it is not your main target vowel; it is only a transition. Look at the musical example to see my suggested time-scale for this:

2. Keeping your awareness of medialisation, sing the example for yourself, and be aware of the change of position in the lips from rounded to neutral as you move into the main target vowel 'ER' [ɜː] or 'URR' [ɝ] (U.S).

3. Now do the same with the word 'yes'. You should pitch the initial 'EE' [iː] and then move quickly into the main target vowel 'eh' [e].

4. Now sing 'romance' and notice what is happening with your tongue as you form the 'r'. The first sound in 'r' at the beginning of a word will be like the schwa 'uh' [ə]. As with the other glides, you should pitch this just before the written beat, and then sing the main vowel on the beat. (See the example below.)

Ro- mance___

Treating the 'r' as a vowel means you can medialise, so prepare this sound with your tongue in the ready position.

You need to treat 'r' in the middle of a word differently. Look at the beginning of *'Unusual Way'* from *A Call from the Vatican* by Maury Yeston:

You will want to be very precise about when you place the 'r' (before

In a   ve -ry un-u - su-al way   one time_   I need - ed you.__

the beat) and aware of the need to come off it quickly, otherwise you are in danger of inserting a syllable that isn't there. So this is a case where you do not want to exaggerate the transition.

You can use the above extract to practise singing transitions.

Problem 4: syllabification of consonants

This is the opposite situation to the one outlined in Problem 3. Here, a written consonant becomes a vowel. A typical example of syllabification occurs when we say 'people'; in speech the final 'l' replaces what would be a vowel. As soon as this process is elongated, we run into a problem: which vowel do we sing? So in Jule Styne's famous song, we are confronted with this problem straight away; it begins, 'People, people, who needs people'. The second, weak syllable of 'people' is sung on a five beat note, and this sequence is repeated a number of times in the song.

Peo -ple_____

The solution is not dissimilar to what we did earlier in *'I Remember'*. On the second syllable of 'people', use the vowel 'ou' [ʊ] and decay into the 'l' [l], pitching it for a couple of beats.

Note that this is also a solution for decaying into the dark 'll' [ɫ], which requires a transition sound as the back of the tongue moves towards the soft palate for the 'll'.

3. Working the consonants

First you have to know how the consonants are made. Opposite is a diagram showing 'placement': where the consonants are made in the vocal tract. You cannot work the consonants harder unless you are doing them properly. If you have trained as an actor or have taken voice lessons, the diagram and subsequent chart will be familiar to you. I find that a lot of singers and dancers have a hazy idea of how consonants are made. This means that they are the relying on the muscular patterns of their habitual speech for performance, which is not enough.

The following chart gives the classification of the 'Consonants of Standard Speech'. The muscles used for each sound are indicated. Sample words are included alongside each category as well as the phonetic symbol.

Take some time to read through this chart. Do not fall into a panic if you are unfamiliar with some of the terminology; it is there to give specific information about how each sound is made. Use the placement terminology diagram as you work through this list: it will help you to focus on the muscular effort required to form the consonants. In practical terms there are three questions to think about:

1. Are the vocal folds vibrating or open (voicing)?
2. Where is the consonant made (place of obstruction)?
3. How is the consonant made (manner)?

If you can answer these questions, you have all the information you need to make the consonants bigger so that they can be heard. The human ear is an amazing organ: so long as it gets enough cues for the sound, it can work it out. When we enlarge the consonants we target the main features of each sound and make them bigger. You should be able to answer the questions above for each sound, using the chart and the diagrams. After that, it's a matter of work. There are exercises for working the consonants at the end of this chapter.

Placement

The places where the vocal tract can be obstructed are numbered.

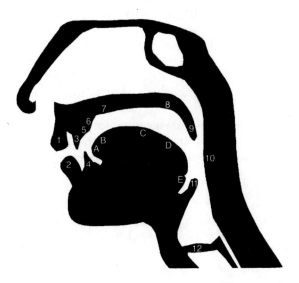

1. Upper lip
2. Lower lip
3. Upper front teeth
4. Lower front teeth
5. Alveolar ridge
6. Postalveolar region
7. Palate
8. Velum (soft palate)
9. Uvula
10. Pharynx
11. Epiglottis
12. Glottis

The places of articulation used in standard speech are 1, 2, 3, 5, 6, 7, 8 and 12.

The letters indicate parts of the tongue: the tip (A), blade (B), front (C), back (D) and root (E).

Consonants of Standard Speech

Bilabial (involving the upper and lower lips)
[p]   voiceless bilabial plosive: **p**eel, a**pp**roach, stoo**p**
[b]   voiced bilabial plosive: **b**ell, tri**b**ute, tu**b**e
[m]   voiced bilabial nasal: **m**arry, ca**m**paign, handso**m**e

Consonants of Standard Speech (continued)

Labiodental (lower lip and upper front teeth)
[f]   voiceless labiodental fricative: **f**ellow, a**f**ter, stu**ff**
[v]   voiced labiodental fricative: **v**ery, a**v**erage, gi**v**e

Labial-velar (upper and lower lips, and the back of the tongue at the area of the velum)
[w]   voiced labial-velar approximant: **w**est, stal**w**art, a**w**ay
[ʍ]   voiceless labial-velar fricative: **wh**at, **wh**ether, a**wh**ile

Dental (the tip of the tongue and the upper teeth)
[θ]   voiceless dental fricative: **th**ink, a**th**lete, tru**th**
[ð]   voiced dental fricative: **th**is, ra**th**er, bli**the**

Alveolar (the blade of the tongue and the alveolar ridge)
[t]   voiceless alveolar plosive: **t**ime, fu**t**ile, ha**t**
[d]   voiced alveolar plosive: **d**eep, a**dd**ition, be**d**
[s]   voiceless alveolar fricative: **s**ip, a**ss**ume, bli**ss**
[z]   voiced alveolar fricative: **z**est, pre**s**ume, head**s**
[l]   voiced alveolar lateral approximant: **l**ast, f**l**our, simi**l**ar
[ɫ]   voiced velarised alveolar lateral approximant: pu**ll**, se**lf**, si**l**ver
[n]   voiced alveolar nasal: **n**either, a**n**tique, fu**n**

Postalveolar (the front of the tongue and the postalveolar ridge)
[ʃ]   voiceless postalveolar fricative: **sh**ift, vi**ci**ous, po**sh**
[ʒ]   voiced postalveolar fricative: bei**ge**, centrifu**ge**, rou**ge**
[tʃ]   voiceless postalveolar affricate: **ch**est, an**c**ient, lur**ch**
[dʒ]   voiced postalveolar affricate: **j**ump, a**dj**acent, ba**dge**
[ɹ]   voiced postalveolar approximant: **r**ed, a**rr**ow, ru**r**al

Palatal (the front of the tongue and the palate)
[j]   voiced palatal approximant: **y**esterday, can**y**on, vine**y**ard

Velar (the back of the tongue and the soft palate)
[k]   voiceless velar plosive: **k**ept, sil**k**en, sha**ck**
[g]   voiced velar plosive: **g**uest, be**g**otten, bi**g**
[ŋ]   voiced velar nasal: si**ng**, li**n**k, Li**n**coln

Glottal (the space between the vocal folds)
[h]   voiceless glottal fricative: **h**ave, a**h**ead, **h**uge
[ʔ]   voiceless glottal plosive: wo', la'er, 'uh-'oh

Problem 1: an up-tempo patter song

Here's a sample problem in which you can explore the level of effort involved in enlarging the consonants if you want your words to be heard in a theatre space. Gilbert and Sullivan were writers of early British Musical Theatre (though they were called operas), and their style was characterised by the patter song – an extremely demanding wordy song – often comic, and delivered at speed. Suppose you had to do a modern version of the patter song – Sondheim's *'Everybody says Don't'* from *Anyone Can Whistle.*

The tempo indicated is fast, and there are a lot of words. You don't want your audience to miss any of them.

> **Everybody says Don't,**
> **Everybody says Don't,**
> **Everybody says Don't, it isn't right,**
> **Don't, it isn't nice.**

1. Speak the lines through once, at your normal speaking pace.

2. Now do the consonants only at a comfortable speed: 'v'–'r'–'b' and so on. (Note that the letter y stands for a vowel in this passage, so leave it out for the moment.) Do not try to make the vowels; they will come anyway when you release the consonants, but don't spend any time on them.

3. Speak the passage again and exaggerate the consonants:

i. allowing twice as much time for all the fricatives, e.g. 'v', 'z', 's';

ii. doubling your effort in making the stopped consonants; the voiceless stops will be stopped for longer, e.g. 't'. There will be a longer build-up in the preparation of voiced stops, e.g. 'b', 'd';

iii. doubling the volume of your nasal consonants wherever they appear in the word, e.g. 'n'.

4. Sing the passage at half speed, or slower if you need it. Don't worry about the volume you normally get from the vowels; just concentrate on the consonants. It will feel weird because you will be stopping the sound for longer than usual on the voiceless consonants, and making the obstruction for longer on the voiced ones.

You might have noticed or experienced the following points when you worked on the patter song:

1. If you are not used to working the consonants this way, it will feel very different to make them diction listener-orientated. You are exaggerating the perceptual cues in each sound for the audience, and it will not feel 'natural'.

2. You probably took more breath than usual, but it 'just happened'. As you articulated your final consonants with energy the voice stopped, and

you were able to recoil automatically with the breath. This is a wonderful device when you are singing a song like this at speed!

3. You can breathe on the aspiration that follows voiceless stops such as 't', 'p', 'k', 's' and 'CH' [tʃ].

4. When you did the voiced consonants you feel as though you were hardly singing the vowel at all. You need to realise that, if you are going to sing in time, the consonants must rob time from the vowels that precede them, making the vowels shorter. You also need to voice your consonants on pitch, but more of that later.

5. If you wanted to make a longer stop on the stops, such as 'don't', you had to make the 'd' before the beat. *With stopped sounds at the beginning of a word, you must rob time from the previous beat (or rest).*

6. In the same way, *with stopped sounds at the end of a word, you must rob time from the note itself.* If you do not do this, you will not be singing in time. You may end up 'back-phrasing' – a ploy used by jazz singers to deliberately delay the beat, and the musical director will assume you want to slow down!

You might have hit some of the following difficulties:

1. Constriction at the larynx. This is an effort issue: when you make an unvoiced consonant, such as 's' or 't', there should be no work in the larynx. We often forget this when singing and introduce constriction. If you are making the consonant with the correct muscles, it is almost impossible to constrict. Check that you are retracted, and that you are not using the vocal folds to stop the breath when you make these sounds.

2. When you made the 't' at the end of the word 'don't', there might have been an explosion of air and an extra vowel 'don-tuh'. This is a common problem. Air is held and then released as we make the stopped sounds. Practise saying the 't' putting more energy into the build-up before you make the sound than after it. When you do release the breath, engage the anchoring muscles inside the mouth and the support around the waistband and the explosion will be more controlled. *With stopped sounds you must control the onset of breath as you release into the vowel that follows*, otherwise you will make too loud an aspirate. The same is true of voiced stops, e.g. 'Don't be afraid', and both categories of consonant at the end of words.

3. A pitch scoop on the voiced sounds 'd' and 'v'. This happens because we normally do the voicing on a low pitch. If you are not careful, you will end up singing that pitch as you do the consonant, and it won't be the right one. Some people make a habit of this and always do the voiced consonant on the octave below the given pitch. This gives rise to pitch slides and scooping which are horrible! Voiced consonants must be pitched on the note that is written. There is a practice exercise for this

problem at the end of this chapter.

All of these points have come out of working on four bars of music! It's a powerful exercise though, and preparation like this will get you through the song with ease. In this exercise you were targeting the features of the consonants and making them bigger. This is how to exaggerate the consonants so that the audience can hear your every word. There's a spin-off that you may have noticed if you were recording yourself or rehearsing this with a pianist: your voice comes out more strongly if you are focusing on the consonants. It always happens, because the consonants demand that you generate a lot of energy.

Problem 2: backpressure on voiced sounds ('v', 'd', 'g', 'j' [dʒ])

Because we are voicing as well as partially stopping the breath to make these sounds, there is a danger in singing that we will back up too much air behind the obstruction of the consonant. This will force the larynx down and could lead to constriction or singing flat. Here's my solution:

1. You will experience the voiced part of a sound as a small grunt at the level of the larynx when you try to pitch on the note. Make this sound at about the same effort level in the larynx as you use for the siren so that it's a really small sound. Above the level of the larynx (at the soft palate, the lips and hard palate), you can use a bigger effort number.

2. Sing the note you need to sing on 'ng' [ŋ] as in the siren. Remember to laugh at the larynx.

3. Keeping your effort level the same, voice the consonant you need to sing, also on the note.

You will find that you can work the consonant quite hard this way without making any backpressure or causing constriction. This is particularly useful if you are singing the above sounds on a high note.

Problem 3: coming off voiced sounds

This work applies to voiced fricatives, and the lateral 'l'. Consider what happens when you are finishing a word, either at the end of a phrase or before a new word. You need to stop the voicing before you do the next sound, or go into a rest. Otherwise you will make another vowel. e.g. 'time-uh-heals-zeverything-uh'. So *as you finish a voiced sound you should also open the vocal folds* as if you were going to breathe. You do not actually have to take a breath; just open the folds. There is an exercise for this at the end of the chapter.

4. Avoiding running words into each other.

You must not run words into each other. This is particularly important when singing a ballad; you don't want to produce a string of well-sung vowels and nonsense words! I want to look at the opening bars of Jerry

Herman's *'Time Heals Everything'* from *Mac and Mabel*, to explore what happens when we sing a ballad. Now, a ballad, of its nature, is sustained. When people want to hear the quality of your singing voice in audition, a ballad is what they ask for. There's usually a good tune, expansive phrases and long notes. Jerry Herman's song is no exception; the melody is simple but memorable and is repeated in a rising sequence. How can you get the audience to really listen to what you are saying when you sing this, rather than being seduced into the melody? Look at the first four lines:

> **Time heals ev'rything, Tuesday, Thursday,**
> **Time heals ev'rything, April, August.**
> **If I'm patient, the break will mend,**
> **And one fine morning the hurt will end.**

Assuming that you have absorbed the work we did earlier, and have practised speaking through all the consonants, now continue with the following:

1. Read the text aloud in an ordinary speech rhythm. Mean what you say as you say it. If you do this, you will instinctively put the commas in, yet I have often heard the first line performed in one breath because that's the way the melody scans. The commas are there, so put them in when you sing!

2. Make sure you stress the all-important word 'ev'rything' by putting a glottal stop at the beginning of it. As well as separating this word from the previous one, it puts a musical and vocal underlining to the word 'everything'. And of course, at this moment in the show, time is not healing everything for Mabel; she is suffering. The glottal gives you an opportunity to signal this to the audience, because when you make a stop in a ballad, the audience will listen.

3. Sing the passage, putting in all the commas and using the glottal onset for words beginning with a vowel (everything, April, August, if, and so on). When you make the commas, don't worry about breathing in; you will automatically do a small recoil when you make the stop. (And here is another opportunity to signal what you are feeling to the audience; silences are wonderful moments that give the audience processing time.)

You don't have to use a glottal onset for every word that begins with a vowel; you can use a simultaneous onset if you prefer a softer attack. In speech it is conventional to insert a glottal before a vowel if the word or syllable is stressed. However, remember that stress is relative: if everything is stressed, then, in effect, nothing is stressed. So whether or not you choose to separate words with a glottal onset is actually an interpretative decision. What is important in singing is that you do not run words into each other, making nonsense of the text, e.g. 'lettus spray' (let us pray); 'inner very yunusual way' (in a very unusual way). *Mark the separation between words in your copy when you are learning a new song.*

Here's a note about singing on 'l'. In Chapter 8 I discussed the importance of medialisation as a way of tuning the vocal tract and mentioned the 'l' as being the only lateral sound in Standard British and US. As a practice exercise, sing the word 'feeling' on one note. You will want to voice the 'l' on pitch without losing the placement of the vowels either side of it. As you move into the 'l' simply drop the tongue from the sides of the teeth (the upper back molars) and keep the tongue fronted. Look back to my example of Jule Styne's *'People'* on page 144 to see how you should treat the dark 'll' [ɫ].

5. *Avoiding distorting sounds*

You should not distort words and syllables. This is a delicate point, and it is the final one of our diction problems. Sometimes the composer sets a long note on an unstressed syllable, which distorts the natural inflection of the word. Writing an unstressed syllable on high note can have the same effect. It is more often a problem in ballads than in up-tempo numbers, because the composer has more opportunity to get caught up in the melody.

Look at *'Someone Like You'* from Frank Wildhorn's *Jekyll and Hyde*, and you will see what I mean.

> **I peer through wind<u>ows</u>,**
> **Watch life go by,**
> **Dream <u>of</u> tomor<u>row</u>**
> **And wonder why.**

The syllables underlined are on long notes and on a rising phrase, so it would be easy to make them stick out in the phrase. I've found that a lot of actors who are sensitive to text, dislike singing ballads for this reason; they feel that they cannot make sense of the text and sing the note-values.

You can, if you use decay. Decay is about sensitivity to word phrasing and inflection. If you stress the strong syllable and decay on the weak one, you will maintain the integrity of the text. You do this by adjusting your volume control; in other words, it is OK to get softer as you sing the second syllable.

The same sort of thing can happen in a phrase on a whole word. The word set to the highest or longest note might be an unimportant one like 'and', 'in' or 'to'. You wouldn't shout these words out in a speech, so make them softer when you sing them. The audience will still be listening because you will be making sense! Here's an example from a very well-known song, '*Somewhere Over the Rainbow*', where we need to use decay.

This famous melody starts with an octave leap; it is a musical picture of the longing expressed through the song. However, it will inevitably lead to loud unstressed syllable if the singer is not careful to use decay. In normal speech there is a drop in volume on the unstressed syllable, so sing it like you'd say it. Remember that high notes are heard as louder by the human ear so '-where' will automatically be louder if you do not decay.

1. Set your volume level first. All dynamic levels are relative. If you want to belt out the song joyously, that is fine; alternatively, you may prefer something more wistful and lyrical. Set your levels accordingly.

2. Make a conscious effort to decrescendo as you approach the top note. Don't just decrescendo on the note; it must happen before you get there.

3. Use the 'm' of 'some' to help you with the decay; you will automatically get a drop in volume on the nasal 'm' because the sound is being filtered through the nose. You want to make sure that as you move back into oral resonance (the 'OO' [uː] of 'where' and the vowel that follows), you don't get a sudden burst of sound. Aim to match the volume of the 'm' with the 'where' and then decay through the rest of the syllable.

One of my happy professional experiences has been working with the National Youth Music Theatre. In 1996 we did a production of John Gay's *The Beggar's Opera* as part of the Edinburgh Festival. The text of *The Beggar's Opera* is dense and wordy. A lot of the songs are fast, being set to dance music of the time, and so diction is a challenge in this piece. I think it's fair to say that the performers bore my badgering and daily consonant work very well! We were very happy with the opening night which took place in a theatre in Kendall. When we transferred to Edinburgh, we hit a problem in the change of acoustic. The singers were not miked, and they noticed the difference immediately; the space was dryer and duller acoustically, and they were getting tired more easily. Since I was responsible in this show for the spoken and sung voice work, I decided that I needed to work the whole company into the new space. What we worked on was diction, not volume. We enlarged the consonants rather than the vowels, and it made an enormous difference. The performers felt they were making contact with the audience through the consonants and noticed that their voices did not tire. I mention this because when you apply the work that follows, you need to be aware that every space you work in is different. I think this is particularly important during auditioning, which takes place without the aid of the sound man, and, often, in a space that has an unkind acoustic. You must use your judgement and adjust accordingly.

You can work the exercise that follows with any sequence of simple vowels from the chart on page 106. Always start with 'EE' [iː] so that you can set the tongue in the ready position.

Exercise 2: CONSONANTS

1. Sing five vowels to each consonant and work through all the consonants listed on the chart on page 142. (Don't sing the glides: 'w', 'r' and 'y'.)
2. Start as slowly as you need and work up the scale.

[diː] [de] [dɑː] [dɔː] [duː]   [diː] [de] [dɑː] [dɔː] [duː]   [diː]

3. Put more effort into the consonants than into the vowels; the consonants should be louder than the vowels.
4. When you are doing voiced consonants, be sure to pitch the voicing on each note of the scale as you go up.
5. When you are doing voiceless consonants, form the sounds well before each beat in the sequence. Do not try to open out much when you sing the vowels, there isn't time.
6. Increase the number of beats and, gradually, the speed, by doing three beats on each note of the scale:

[diː diː diː de de de dɑː dɑː dɑː dɔː dɔː dɔː duː]   [diː diː diː de de de ...]

You will find this easier to do if you increase your effort for the build-up to the first note in each of the triplets. The other two sounds will bounce off that first effort.

7. Really pay attention when doing this exercise, to where you are doing the work and how. Pay attention to the 'point of obstruction' where the consonant is made, and to the breath stream. Consider the following examples:

a. Making an 'f' requires work in the lips and friction in the breath stream;

b. Making a 'k' requires work in the soft palate (velum) and tongue. The breath is first held, then released;

c. Making a 'z' requires work in the tongue against the alveolar ridge. There is some friction in the breath;

d. Making an 'l' requires work in the tongue on the alveolar ridge and the breath is continuous.

8. Take a breath whenever you need it in this exercise. It should be easy to recoil.

9. You should be laughing silently at the larynx throughout.

Exercise 2 will help you to build muscularity in your consonants and teach you to pitch them on the note. You can follow it up with any number of tongue-twisters or a passage from a song. A fun exercise from my US colleague Dr Steve Chicurel is to sing nonsense words to the tune of *William Tell*, such as 'Johnny has a head like a ping-pong ball!' You can make up your own phrases to use as warm-ups.

Exercise 3: COMING OFF VOICED CONSONANTS

The formation of vowels and consonants requires complex activity in the vocal tract; when coming off voiced consonants it is important to separate the effort in the articulators from the work in the larynx.

1. Practise the aspirate and simultaneous onsets from Chapter 2, doing several onsets in a row. Notice that, to stop and start the sound, you are off-setting (coming out of voice) as well as onsetting. You do this by opening the vocal folds and – usually – breathing in again after you have made the sound.

2. Now do the same with the following voiced fricatives: 'v'–'v', 'th'–'th', 'z'–'z', and so on.

3. If you are not careful, and one of these sounds appears at the end of a word, you will produce an involuntary vowel sound as you release the consonant, (e.g. 'love-uh'). To avoid this, you must co-ordinate three things:

i. Maintain the shape of the consonant (point of obstruction) until you have finished the note.

ii. Come off voice by opening your vocal folds.

iii. If appropriate, stop the breath stream from the abdomen.

This rule also applies to the nasals and to the lateral 'l'. You are now performing is 'offset of voice'.

Exercise 4: ANALYSE YOUR OWN SONG

This is a wonderful exercise that enables you to work out which sound you are singing at any point in the song. It's a great way to learn words and to put you in touch with the different muscular efforts involved in forming the words before you even start singing. This process should be part of your preparation process when you are learning a new song.
You should choose your own song (preferably a ballad for the first time you do this), but, to start you off, I will take you through the process using the opening bars of *'Time Heals Everything'*.
Look at the words of the song again and speak them slowly, taking time with every sound:

Time heals ev'rything, Tuesday, Thursday,
Time heals ev'rything, April, August.
If I'm patient, the break will mend,
And one fine morning the hurt will end.

1. How many sounds are there in each word? For instance, in 'time' you have a total of four sound targets [taɪm]; in 'hurt', there are three [hɜːt] or [hɝːt] (US). Write in the numbers of sounds under each word, putting the phonetics in if you are familiar with them.
2. If you are not good at phonetics, underline every voiced sound so that you know to pitch it when you start singing.
3. Mark in the glottal stops you will need in any places where you need to stop the voice at the end of a word, e.g. 'Everything' will need a glottal stop. (In the example opposite an apostrophe indicates a glottal stop.)
4. Also mark in any places where the voice stops at the end of a word because there is a voiceless consonant. It's amazing how often singers will try to continue voicing at these points when there is a melody to sing. Put a stop mark (e.g. /) for the final sounds of, e.g., 'break' and 'hurt'.
5. Now mark in any sounds using the ˜ that require you to open the nasal port, e.g. 'patie<u>n</u>t'.

   The song lyrics are shown overleaf with all of these markings. Note that the bracketed numbers are for standard US pronunciation where it differs from British.

6. Sing the song at thinking speed, putting in all the things you have marked in for yourself. Sing the song at a comfortable pitch as if to yourself. Work all the sounds in each syllable as you do so.
7. Sing the song slowly at written pitch, still at thinking speed, so that you can pay attention. Notice if there are any sounds that seem more

Tĩme heals 's'ev-'ry-thiñg, Tues-day, Thurs-day,
4   5   2   2   3   4   3   3(4) 3

Tĩme heals 'ev'-ry-thiñg, 'A-pril, 'Au-gust./
4   5   2   2   3   2   4   1   4

'If 'I'm̃ pa-tieñt/, the break/ will mẽñd,
2   3 2   4   2   5   3   4

'Añd oñe fiñe m̃or-ñiñg the hurt/ will 'eñd.
3   2   4   2(3) 3   2   3(4) 3   3

difficult to make at the written pitch. Have a look through the problems
section in this chapter to see if you can identify why this is happening.
8. Sing the song up to speed, still working the diction.

Exercise 5: LISTENING

Read the words and listen to a performance of Rodgers and
Hammerstein's *'If I Loved You'*, to the first half of Sondheim's *'So Many
People'*, and to the whole of *'Someone Like You'* mentioned earlier. Listen
to the setting of the words and notice where you would need to use
decay.

Doing the work outlined in this chapter is fundamental to your job as a
communicator. When you start to work the consonants, amazing things
happen, and they are 90% of the job of acting! As you work the
consonants, you commit to the text and automatically connect with the
underlying meaning. And you will find the audience are with you all the
way!

Chapter 12

Creating voice qualities

Every time you sing, you will be making some kind of voice quality whether you are conscious of it or not. But you don't have just 'one voice'; you can create a range of voice qualities by adjusting the muscle groups in the vocal tract. Now that you are technically secure and have control over the components for vocalising, you can learn these adjustments and create different voice qualities.

Singing is learned behaviour. Depending on your training (whether it is formal or informal) and your habitual speech patterns, you will have a voice quality that feels natural to you. This is your vocal set-up. You need to be aware of what your set-up is before you can change it, just as in body work you need to find neutral before beginning to change physicality for characterisation. So in singing, learning how to change your vocal set-up enables you to change vocal characterisation. This is very empowering.

Jo Estill has identified six voice qualities (speech, falsetto, cry, twang, opera and belt), all of which are used in theatre singing. Some of these voice qualities are complex, and it would not be appropriate for me to teach you them through the book. Each one has a specific set-up in the vocal tract, as well as 'dos' and 'don'ts' for safe application. If you want to learn the voice qualities properly, you should go to a workshop or training course that can offer them, or work with a teacher who is familiar with the Estill model. For the purposes of this book, I will be discussing the voice qualities and how they are used in theatre singing. In my opinion you cannot get through a career in musical theatre without having some knowledge of voice qualities. I will then give you the parameters for changing voice quality so that you can hear and identify them for yourself. Once you have this information you will find that you are able to create most of the qualities I'm about to outline provided that you have mastered the vocal tasks set out in the book up to this point. Having grasped the concept of voice qualities, you will realise that there are many, many vocal colours available to you, enabling you to change characterisation and depict different psychological states with your voice. You will also be more marketable as a performer because you will be able to encompass a variety of musical styles. I will talk more about this in Chapter 13 'The act of singing'.

How voice qualities are used

1. **Speech quality**. This is the musical theatre version of operatic recitative. You need it for the verse part of a set song (e.g., 'When you're awake, the things you think, come from the dreams you dream.'). You also need it for narrative, direct communication, for patter songs and point numbers: all those moments when you are not actually in song mode but have notes to sing! Both *Les Misérables* and *Miss Saigon*, which are through-composed (that is with no dialogue), require you to produce speech quality. A great deal of Sondheim's music requires speech quality in both the solo and ensemble singing – *Into the Woods*, *Merrily We Roll Along* – and this quality is also a feature of pop singing, where it is often mixed with twang.

2. **Falsetto quality**. This can be used by both men and women, and it is needed for moments of reflection, intimacy, and uncertainty. You might use falsetto quality when talking to a loved one (e.g., the opening bars of *A Call from the Vatican*). Jean Valjean famously uses it in the prayer *'God on High'* in *Les Misérables*, and it is also entirely suitable for the beginning of a ballad such as *'What More Can I Say?'* in *Falsettoland*. Falsetto quality is something you use in parts of a song; it is rarely used for a whole number but it is enormously effective as a vocal colour.

3. **Cry quality.** When you are singing ballads your sound needs to warm and approachable. This is cry quality. It involves tilting the thyroid, which gives you vibrato and sweetness of tone. The juvenile lead often has to sing the ballads, e.g., Amalia in *She Loves Me*, with *'Will He Like Me?'*, and *'Vanilla Ice-cream'*, which also borders on opera. Cry quality denotes depth and romantic passion; think of *'A Heart Full of Love'*, or the beginning of *'I'd Give My Life for You'*. Maria in *West Side Story* would use cry quality a lot and even opera quality in moments of high passion. Cry quality is absolutely necessary for a lot of the romantic roles in the classic book musicals: *Carousel*, *Showboat*, *Oklahoma!*

4. **Twang.** This is a wonderful mixer as well as a voice quality in its own right. Twang 'ups the ante'! Twang is often indicated in character roles; you cannot do Ado Annie without twang. Twang can be frenetic and neurotic, like Johanna in *Sweeney Todd* and Anne in *A Little Night Music*. Twang can also indicate coarseness or a hard-boiled quality in a character: Thenardier in *Les Misérables*, or a pimp in *The Life*.

5. **Opera quality.** Even opera quality is used quite a lot in musical theatre: the opera cats and Deuteronomy use it in *Cats*, and you need some element of opera quality for most roles in *Phantom of the Opera*. Sweeney Todd sings in opera quality and practically every other voice quality in the course of the musical; Pirelli also sings in opera quality. You cannot sing *Carmen Jones* without some opera quality, and a lyric musical

such as *Showboat* also demands an operatic sound.

6. **Belt quality**. Belting is prevalent throughout the West End and on Broadway. You will definitely enhance your chances of work if you can produce a belt as well as sing 'legit'. I teach all of my students to belt as a matter of course. In the UK, unless you are specifically going for the role of Cosette in *Les Misérables*, you may not get past the second round of auditioning if you cannot belt; it is a requirement for the show. Any of the pop or gospel musicals, such as *Rent* or *Smokey Joe's Café* will also require expertise in belting.

MAKING THE VOICE QUALITIES

I began by introducing the notion of vocal set-up for each quality. Let's start by looking at the parameters that define a change of set-up. You have already learned how to control each of these structures.

1. The larynx. Is the larynx high, low or neutral? What is its posture? Is it tilted in the thyroid, the cricoid, or neutral?

2. The vocal folds. Are they working hard (thick), minimally (thin), or not closing (stiff)?

3. The resonators. What is the condition of the nasal port? Is the twanger on or off?

4. Effort levels. Some voice qualities are harder work than others. You will need to know where you are doing the work, and how hard. High-energy voice qualities such as belting and opera require a higher degree of effort in the silent laugh posture in order to avoid constriction. You must also consider the level of effort in the anchoring muscles. How hard are you working in the head and neck, in the torso?

These are the factors involved in changing voice quality. Each quality is then defined by the state of the structures outlined above. Jo Estill has called these different states 'recipes'. I shall examine the voice qualities in pairs so that you can spot the differences and similarities more easily.

Speech and Falsetto

These two are the qualities of 'conversational singing'. Here are their common factors:

1. The larynx is not tilted in either quality: the position is neutral as in everyday speech. The height of the larynx is also neutral, though you should allow for adjustment in the larynx as you approach high notes.

2. The nasal port is closed, and there is no twang in either quality. However, you can add twang to boost your speech quality.

3. The anchoring will be relaxed in these qualities; in speech quality

you can support the work in the vocal folds by anchoring at certain points in your range.

The difference between these two qualities is in the level of work in the vocal folds. In falsetto quality, the breath is free-flowing with no resistance in the vocal folds; the sound will be breathy. In speech quality, there is more resistance in the vocal folds and a longer closed phase.

Speech quality works best in the bottom of the range for women and towards the upper mid-range for men. (This is because men generally have a bigger larynx and therefore longer and thicker vocal folds than women.) Speech quality is comfortable up to E or F above middle C (real pitch for both gender). You can take it higher, but it has to be done with care.

Falsetto quality has less risks associated with it. The only problems you will encounter is that it does not work well at the bottom of the range; the sound just disappears. Also, it is not a loud quality. If you are not using a microphone (head mike or standing) you should change your voice quality to gain more volume.

Cry and Twang

Here are their common factors:

1. Both qualities involve a tilted thyroid.

2. Because of the tilting, the vocal folds are stretched thinner than in speech quality. In both qualities you will have vibrato.

3. The set-up for both these qualities starts with the siren; the vocal folds are thin, the sound is quiet and the thyroid cartilage is tilted as in whining or maiowing.

4. Because of the effort involved in laryngeal tilting and in tightening the twanger, it is essential in both qualities that you are well retracted.

Here are the differences:

1. In cry quality, the nasal port is closed; nothing is coming down the nose. In twang, you can choose to have the nasal port open or closed; your sound will be louder when the port is closed.

2. The effort level in cry quality is higher than in twang; you will need a degree of anchoring in the head and neck. You may also need to use torso anchoring as the airflow for cry quality is very low. You do not need to be anchored in twang.

3. You can produce a version of cry quality with a lowered larynx, which is called 'sob'. In twang, you don't want to lower the larynx. Twang is louder than cry, because of the tightened AES.

I have found many students running into problems with breath use when attempting nasal twang because they do not have control over the nasal port. This is because the breath is being directed into two places in the vocal tract: the nose and the mouth. The student then becomes used to pushing air, and this can result in a breathy, pushed tone. Nasal twang should be a choice, not a default.

Belting and Opera

You may be a bit surprised to see these two qualities being dealt with together. In fact, they have a lot in common as they are both high-energy voice qualities involving control over a number of structures in the vocal mechanism. Hence they are called complex voice qualities.

1. In both qualities, the vocal folds are thick and the closed phase is long. In other words, there is a high degree of work in the vocal folds.

2. Both qualities include twang in their set-up.

3. A high effort level in retraction, a wide vocal tract, and high effort in the anchoring is required for both.

Here are the differences:

1. The larynx is low for opera, and high for belting.

2. The thyroid is tilted for opera; in belting the cricoid is tilted.

3. There is more work in the vocal folds for belting than in opera.

Some people get very excited when they hear about the voice qualities. They often realise that they have been using some of them already by ear, and are eager to learn how to use them better. Others, especially singers who have been trained by the 'right and wrong sound' method, are sometimes terrified to hear that there is more than one way of doing things! Having read and worked through the book, I hope you are in the former category.

How do you make these qualities? The simplest way for me to show you is via song exercises. You should work the following exercise sequences with a tape recorder so that you can hear the different sounds you are making as you create the voice qualities. When you play it back to yourself, don't worry if you don't like the sound; it may not be what you are used to hearing, but that doesn't mean it is wrong. All of the qualities I have outlined can be made safely *provided they are done properly*.

In Chapter 9 we used the song *'Amazing Grace'* to practise twanging. You now know that twang is identified as a voice quality, and I want to compare it with speech, falsetto and cry qualities with the following exercises.

Exercise 1: STEPS TO SPEECH QUALITY

There is no tilt in speech quality, so we will not start with the siren as we did in Chapter 9.

1. In spoken voice, practise doing a few glottal onsets, first on 'uh-oh', and then on single vowels: 'EE' [iː] to 'OO' [uː]. This will give you the set-up for speech quality.

2. Continue speaking, not singing, and say the vowels again, holding them a little longer than before so that you can feel thicker folds and a longer closed phase.

3. In the same mode, speak the words, this time beginning to elongate the words a little more than for normal speech, so that you are intoning.

4. Now speak the first two words (or syllables) of each phrase and sing the rest.

A - maz - ing____   grace,   how   sweet   the   sound

You will find this easier if you pitch close to your speaking voice.

Watchpoints:

i. This will feel more like speak-singing than singing if you are not used to doing it, but you must nevertheless be retracted.

ii. Your vocal folds are closed for longer in this quality than in cry and twang qualities. This means there will be more resistance to the breath and less air-flow. You should still release the abdominal wall and do a recoil breath at the end of each phrase (or whenever you need to breathe).

iii. You may have difficulty reaching the highest notes of the phrase. This is because speech quality works best in the lower part of the range for women and up to mid-range for men. Do not strain for the high notes; let the volume decrease and use some anchoring in the head and neck as you approach these notes.

iv. The high notes will also be easier if you allow your larynx to rise.

Exercise 2: STEPS TO FALSETTO QUALITY

Falsetto quality is the easiest quality of all and requires very little effort. Below are the opening lines of a well-known song *'The Way You Look Tonight'* by Jerome Kern and Dorothy Fields. It needs to be sung in the style of Fred Astaire or Bing Crosbie.

1. Try singing it. You will find this easier if you rehearse it above your speech range.

2. In Chapter 2 we looked at three ways of starting the sound, including

the aspirate onset (pages 16-17). Do this now, using the fast aspirate, and initiate the tone with an 'h' before each vowel in the song.

Some day when I'm awf'ly low,
When the world is cold,
I will feel a glow just thinking of you,
And the way you look tonight.
Oh, but you're lovely, with your smile so warm,
And your cheek so soft,
There is nothing for me but to love you,
Just the way you look tonight.

3. In Chapter 7, we did an awareness exercise to see if you were resisting the breath (page 69). It's a characteristic of falsetto quality that there is very little resistance to the breath. You should not be pushing the air, but you will be making an 'easy' breathy tone.
4. Using the vowel 'OO' [uː], sing the melody of the song, initiating the tone every so often with 'h' so that you stay in falsetto quality. Notice that you are using a lot of air: the navel is going towards the backbone as you use the airflow to set off vibrations in the vocal folds. Sometimes this can be drying, but with practice you can monitor the amount of breath you need to make the sound, and you will lose the dryness.
5. Notice that you are not anchored in this voice quality and that there is no tilt in the larynx.
6. Having found your voice quality on 'OO' [uː], speak the words using the same vocal set-up. It may not be like your habitual speaking voice, but that doesn't matter. The point is to notice how it feels.
7. Now sing the song with the words, still in falsetto quality. Depending on where in your range you have pitched the song, you'll notice that the sound is quieter at the bottom of the range and louder at the top. That's the way it is unless you change voice quality.

Exercise 3: STEPS TO CRY QUALITY

Work with 'Amazing Grace'.
1. Begin by sirening the melody as sirening gives you most of the set-up for cry quality. Check that you are doing this with a tilted thyroid (miaow or whine sensation).Then add the following.
2. Anchor the head and neck, and keep the neck wide. You should be retracted with a high effort number (see Chapter 7, pages 69-71). Also use the palato pharyngeus muscle (see Chapter 6, page 62).
3. Anchor the torso a little to stabilise the breathing (see Chapter 7, pages 74-5).

4. With these extra factors in place, miren the song, mouthing the words but keeping the 'ng' [ŋ] siren at the back of the mouth.

5. Sing the song on the vowels only, making sure that the nasal port is closed.

6. Finally, sing the song with the words.

A variation of this is to use 'sob', in which case the larynx will be lowered. The following step can be added between steps 2 and 3.

Instead of using the yawn-sigh manoeuvre that we used in Chapter 3 (page 23) to lower the larynx, you can try silently sobbing as you exhale. If you assume this posture of deep mourning in the larynx, you will be holding it down. It is a very unnatural posture that requires a lot of effort in the extrinsic muscles of the larynx. Sob quality will be even softer than cry because of the lowered larynx.

When I'm teaching cry quality, a student will often ask if it is meant to be such hard work. Yes it is. That's how you create a 'beautiful' sound.

Exercise 4: COMPARING CRY AND TWANG

Sing *Amazing Grace* in twang quality as we did in Chapter 9.

Record yourself singing the song in twang and then in cry qualities. Although there are common factors in the set-up for these two, they sound very different. Notice *where* you feel the difference in order to make these two voice qualities – this is very important. Many musical theatre singers experience difficulties when they are asked to change their style of singing if they do not know how to do it properly. You now have some idea of how to move from Julie Jordan in *Carousel* to the Patsy Cline musical!

Exercise 5: COMPARING EFFORT LEVELS FOR SPEECH, TWANG AND CRY

1. As we also sang *Amazing Grace* using speech quality, let's now compare this with twang and cry.

i. Go over the steps to making speech quality, then sing the whole song.

ii. Notice that your sense of effort is quite different. With twang and cry, you do not feel the effort in the vocal folds. In speech quality you will feel as if you are singing 'on the voice', because the work is in the vocal folds. This is not wrong, just different.

2. Let's do some negative practice to find out what it is like to do too much work in the vocal folds. In this case you would be 'driving the voice'.

i. Set up the speech quality by intoning the words as you did earlier.

ii. Now move into singing the notes, but this time ask yourself to sing louder without increasing the effort anywhere else in the body (in other words, no anchoring, no extra work in the breath, no extra retraction).

iii. Pretty soon your voice will start to hurt if you go on like this, and you are likely to constrict as the vocal folds co-opt the false vocal folds in their efforts to increase volume. This is not a good thing to do, so when you are working with speech quality, monitor the effort level in your vocal folds so that it feels comfortable. If you want to increase volume in this quality you will need to either add twang, or anchor, or change voice quality.

3. Listen to the recording you have made so far. Notice that each quality has its own 'feel'. Of course, it would be unusual to sing a whole song in just one quality, but you have an idea now of how changing quality can effect the mood of the song. Remember that your response to the qualities is subjective (just as your audience's will be), but that *you have created the qualities objectively*. To put it another way, the change in quality will denote a change of emotion even if you do not feel it yourself – you are acting with your voice.

Exercise 6: COMPARING SPEECH AND FALSETTO

Of course, you could compare these two using *'Amazing Grace'* if you wanted to, but I suspect you can only take so much of one song! Here's a great way to compare speech and falsetto qualities in spoken voice.

1. Revise 'Steps to falsetto quality'. Then speak the lines of *'The Way You Look Tonight'* in a breathy falsetto quality. In the UK this may call to mind the revamped voice of Margaret Thatcher in the late 1980's (particularly if you lower your larynx as well). Members of the caring profession, speech therapists and counsellors often use falsetto, so you might know someone you could use as a role model in this area. (Remember that men can speak in falsetto mid-way through their range as well as at the top.)

2. When you reach 'and the way you look', drop suddenly into speech quality, initiating the 'and' with a glottal onset to make sure you do so. You may find it helpful to take a drop in pitch as you do this, though it is not essential.

3. Notice the difference in airflow. You will use far less air in making the speech quality because there is more closure. Can you feel this closure at fold level? That is the main difference between falsetto and speech. You may also experience a crack or yodel as you flip from falsetto to speech quality. This is quite characteristic of making a sudden change from one to the other, and it is used in Rock 'n' Roll, and Country and Western singing.

4. The song goes through an octave, so if you now pitch it comfortably in your range, you should be able to compare singing in these two qualities.

5. Record yourself doing this and make a note of the difference in feel; the falsetto quality is more intimate, the speech quality, more direct.

Opera quality

It is not the objective of this book to teach you to sing operatically. Indeed, I feel strongly that an operatic training is inappropriate for theatre singing. I mentioned above the difficulties that musical theatre singers may encounter in meeting the needs of different vocal styles, something that is essential if you are to remain in employment. In my experience, these difficulties commonly arise from trying to create a more contemporary sound with a classical singer's set-up. Actually, this is dangerous, just as dangerous as it can be to attempt demanding operatic roles without proper training. With this in mind, I want to examine the operatic set-up.

For opera quality, you need thick folds. The thyroid is tilted and the larynx lowered. You are fully anchored and the twanger is tightened. You could say that opera is a combination of three voice qualities: speech, cry and twang. A tilted thyroid and lowered larynx are hallmarks of opera quality and are instantly recognisable. This quality requires complex activity and muscular balance in the vocal tract. For example, normally we do not twang with a low larynx. Assuming that they can achieve a good, healthy speech quality, if I want a more operatic sound from my students, I ask them to do the following:

1. Use 'sob' to tilt and lower the larynx; this combines speech and cry (or sob).

2. Anchor for tone and power.

3. Add twang for brightness.

A student of mine who was a wonderful jazz and soul singer was called to audition for *Carmen Jones*. He had done a number of West End shows but felt very unconfident about the operatic sound needed for this particular show. He was asked to learn the Toreador's song *'Stand Up and Fight'*. I invented the above recipe for him so that he could create the right sound. At the recall he was offered him the job and the panel remarked that 'they didn't know he could sing like that!' You may like to try the above recipe to get a feel for the operatic set-up. Try *'Stand Up and Fight'* (men) or *'Habanera (Dat's Love)'* (women).

Belting

I cannot tell you how many times I have had people walk into my studio saying, 'I need to belt, but I can only sing in my head voice!' All too often I am called to do a repair job on people who have been trying to belt, who did not understand how to do it properly, and who damaged their voices. You can quickly end up with swollen vocal folds or nodules if you are belting eight shows a week with an unsafe technique. For this reason, I will not be teaching you how to belt in the book. You cannot learn belting from a book; you need to work at it with somebody who understands how the voice is set up for belting. Jo Estill has done more research than anybody into this subject, and those of us who have worked with Jo have all found her information on belting invaluable.

What is Belting? Let me tell you first what it is not.

1. Belting is not 'chest voice'. Chest voice (if we must speak of it at all) is generally acknowledged to stop at E/F above middle C and is usually characterised by thick folds and a low larynx. If you try to push your chest voice up beyond this point you are taking risks with your voice. Belting is high larynx and thick folds.

2. Belting and twang are not the same thing, though many people confuse them. Belting is much louder than twang because there is more work in the vocal folds and a high degree of anchoring in the body.

3. Belting is not a loud version of opera quality. You cannot learn to belt using the classical singer's set-up, which is based on a tilted thyroid. In belting you are tilting the cricoid. (See Chapter 3 pages 26-7 for the awareness exercise on cricoid tilt.)

Belting is not harmful if you are doing it right. Jo Estill has described it as 'happy yelling'. Belting is actually a very natural thing for us to do with our voices. Children are belting all the time as they yell to each other in the playground.

Exercise 7: PREPARATION FOR BELTING

We could define belting as a combination of speech and twang qualities with the body fully anchored, the neck widened and a tilted cricoid. Tilting the cricoid enables us to sing at high pitches and to keep the vocal folds thick. Belting starts where speech quality ends (F above middle C, and above, though in some voices, it is higher).

1. The larynx is high in belting. Raise the larynx as you prepare a belt note (see Chapter 3, pages 23-4).
2. You need to be fully retracted in belting. Use a high effort number in your silent laugh and widen the neck as well. (Use the part sit-up described in Chapter 7, pages 70-1.)
3. The head, neck and face should be fully anchored.
4. The tongue is high.
5. The twanger is tightened. (This will make your belt sound louder.)
6. The breath is high. This is the only time you take a clavicular breath. (See Chapter 3, page 26.) The clavicular breath will help keep the larynx high and help reduce your airflow. The vocal folds have a very long closed phase in belting, and you do not want to push air through the belt.

7. When you are belting, it will feel as though you are 'not using the breath'. This is because your vocal folds are doing a lot of the work.

Exercise 8: EFFORT FOR BELTING

1. Put a finger on your larynx and siren silently up to a high note. Notice that your larynx has raised. Stay there.
2. Now take an upper chest breath as though gasping in surprise.
3. You will probably close the vocal folds as you do this; hold this feeling.
4. The tongue should be in an 'EE' [iː] position.
5. Widen the neck by pushing the fist against the forehead (see Chapter 7). Now lift the chin a little so that the head tilts back very slightly. This helps tilt the cricoid.
6. Anchor the head neck and torso fully.
7. Release the vocal folds and breathe just a little in and out, but keep the chest high.
8. Now run a check list:
   i. Are you retracted?
   ii. Can you chew with the jaw and release the facial muscles?
   iii. Can you walk around, holding this degree of effort?

Now you have some idea of the effort level required of the body in belting! It is the most high-energy quality you can create in your voice. If you are belting or trying to belt, check through the above and see if you are using these strategies; you will need them. If you are not and your belt is not working for you, then you should seek the advice of a good teacher.

You can belt as high as your range will allow, once you know what you are doing. You can hear gospel singers belting high A (women) and D a 9th above middle C (men). If your belt voice only goes up to A above middle C (women), the chances are you are not belting but 'chesting'. Women's voices in musical theatre need to be able to belt C, D and E (over an octave above middle C) depending on your type of voice. Men need to be able to belt up to G above middle C (baritones) and between high B and C for tenors. I often find that men's voices can go higher in belt mode than they might otherwise.

People do belt naturally if they are physically strong and have had no classical training. As belting has come into our popular music culture, more and more people are accepting it as a sound. I find that younger students are doing it more easily unless someone has told them that they shouldn't. It really is a question of habitual voice use; if you have been brought up to use your voice as a loud instrument, the chances are that you will not find it too difficult to belt. I can think of one female student who studied with me at drama school with her belt voice already working. This was long before I understood about belting myself, and I could not understand how my student was making this sound. Later she told me that she had always belted; her family came from the East End of London and she had been brought up singing music hall songs. For her, belting was a natural extension of this voice use.

Despite years of musicals in the West End and on Broadway that require belting, I still see students and professionals who have been told that belting is bad for you. This is still happening on drama training courses. So I would just like to say:

1. Belting is perfectly healthy if done properly. Learn the correct set-up.

2. Belting will not ruin your 'head voice'.

3. Classical singers can learn to belt, and anyone can learn to sing opera quality.

Song assignment 1: BELTING

Find a song that requires only one or two notes in belt to begin with. This is particularly important if you are unfamiliar with belting. Some of you will already be belting; if so, use this assignment and the awareness exercise above to check your set-up for belting.

Women might try one of the following:

- the final sequence of *'I'm in Love with a Wonderful Guy'* (mezzo) from *South Pacific*;
- the refrain of *'Don Juan'* (mezzo), *Smokey Joe's Café*;
- the bridge section up to the word 'atmosphere' of *'Quiet Thing'* (mezzo), *Flora the Red Menace*;
- the section beginning 'only darkness and pain' from *'Daddy's Song'* (soprano or mezzo), *Ragtime*;
- the 'Albert' sequence from *'I Think I May Want to Remember Today'* (soprano), *Starting Here, Starting Now*;
- the section beginning 'I've got one night only' from *'One Night Only'* (soprano), *Dream Girls*.

Men could try:

- the section beginning 'they're called Bui-Doi' from *'Bui-Doi'* (tenor), *Miss Saigon*;
- the section beginning 'while the bass is sounding' in *'Those Magic Changes'* (tenor), *Grease*;
- the last two pages of *'What am I Doing?'* (tenor or high baritone), *Closer Than Ever*;
- the section beginning 'years, years too long' from *'The Games I Play'* (baritone), *Falsettos*;
- the build-up to the end of *'I Don't Remember Christmas'* (bass), *Starting Here, Starting Now*.

Choose the passage you want to work on and ask yourself the following questions as you rehearse:

1. What is happening just before you belt? What voice quality are you in? Remember that you will need to change your set-up if you are in a voice quality that is opposite to belt, such as falsetto or cry. Much the easiest way to approach the belt is via speech quality or twang, or a combination of both.

2. Is the larynx high or low ? It needs to be high. If not, raise it using by using the sequence described in Chapter 3, page 26, for tilting the cricoid.

3. Where is the tongue? It must be in the ready position, and the vowel you are singing medialised. Please do not belt with a low flat tongue! (See Chapter 8, pages 103-7.)

4. How hard are you working at retraction? There is greater danger of constricting in belting; assist your effort levels in retracting the false vocal folds by widening the neck.

5. Are you fully anchored in head, neck and torso? Pay particular attention to your level of torso anchoring, which is essential for belting.

6. Is the twanger tightened? Twang is part of the recipe for belt and gives the sound extra 'ring'.

7. Is there air being pushed through the belt? Remember that you need hardly any breath to belt, so make sure you do not push air to start the note. Practise your belt notes with a glottal onset or a 'y' [j] (simultaneous onset) to eliminate the air.

8. What is your body posture? If you are anchored, your lats will be contracted and your chest slightly raised. Below this you will need to unlock the knees and tuck the tail of the spine under. Now look at your head and neck posture. You can raise the chin in belting, but the head should not be poked forward; the head is held and braced backwards. This helps you to tilt the cricoid and is a characteristic posture for belting.

Commercial voice qualities

If you are going up for the commercial musicals you need to be able to move from '50's Rock 'n' Roll (*Buddy* and *Smokey Joe's Café*) through the '60's and '70's (*Saturday Night Fever*) to contemporary styles (*Rent*).

As a general guideline, most commercial styles require a high larynx and twang. The same applies to the pop recording industry (Kate Bush sings with a high larynx, and Alanis Morrisette, Celine Dion, and Boyzone with twang). The pop style demands that you change voice quality frequently, sometimes mid-note and mid-phrase. And the vowels are perceptually flatter, and often nasalised.

Abusive voice qualities

Sometimes actors make a choice to use an abusive voice quality to portray their vocal characterisation. Two roles for which I've heard actors do this are Judas in *Jesus Christ Superstar*, and Magenta in *The Rocky Horror Show*. I want to stress here that not every performer who sings these roles abuses their voice, but unfortunately film and cast recordings do exist in which you can quite clearly hear constriction and heavy rasp in the sound. How can you avoid this when Magenta needs to sound weird, and Judas hysterical and obsessive? I believe what is needed in preparing this type of character is to start working objectively. When we are unhappy, stressed, hysterical, or 'off-the-wall' we naturally constrict. You do not want to sing these roles with this aspect of the characterisation in your voice – you will not last eight shows a week! Work out, instead, which voice qualities you can create to best portray the psychological make-up of your character. You can always find a sound that will do the work for you rather than you tearing your voice apart as you go through the emotional angst of the character each night.

Now that you know about voice qualities and have some idea of the changes need to access them, do some listening. Listen to three different vocal artists, choosing one that you do not particularly like. From the work we you have done in this chapter, try to work out which voice qualities they are using, and notice your response to them. Are the qualities you hear appropriate to the character, the style of music, and the emotions portrayed in the song?

Song assignment 2: WHOSE SONG IS IT ANYWAY?

Do this with a friend or group of friends. It's an exercise in imagination, in listening and in vocal control.

1. You take it in turns to sing the same song (or group of songs if you think you'll get bored with the same one). You should be confident with the notes and the words – preferably off the page.
2. After hearing the song through, your partner asks you to start it again using a specific voice quality.
3. At a suitable point in the song, your partner asks you to change voice quality; again at another change-point, and so on, until you reach the end of the song.
4. Discuss the effect the changes in voice quality had, and whether or not they represent stylistic and character choices that you feel are appropriate for the song.

In a second version of the exercise your partner would ask you to sing the song in different styles, say:

i. portraying different characters, changing age, status and personal history;

ii. with different dramatic intentions.

Your partner's job will be to identify which voice qualities you are using in order to effect the changes; yours will be to use your imagination and instinct as an actor to help you in your choices.

Voice qualities are the vocal equivalent of physical transformation. If you are going to act with your voice, you will need them. Having a range of voice qualities also makes you more marketable. There are so many different styles of musical around at the moment that you may need to be able to change your vocal set-up in order to get work. What I have shown you in this chapter is only the tip of the iceberg. You can probably see that it is possible to add ingredients to the voice qualities I've described and make something different again. There's another major advantage. If you know what you did to make a sound, you can do it again and again, eight times a week for a year at a time. That is technique!

Chapter 13

The act of singing

When you are preparing the text of your song, you are considering both the words and the music. Decisions you ultimately make about your performance will be a balance between these two. An actor who blagues his way through a song by talking it roughly on pitch is not serving the music. A singer who makes a string of impressive noises without communicating the meaning of the words is just playing an instrument. There are also the physical implications to be considered that are part of the characterisation and method of song delivery. Song interpretation is a book in itself, and there are a number on this aspect theatre singing. I can recommend David Craig's *On Singing On Stage* for those of you who may wish to do further reading. The guidelines I'm about to give assume that you have done at least some training as an actor. They allow for you to do your character research and preparation in exactly the way that you would normally do in a play. You will see that, in song preparation, there are additional factors to be considered. These are the tasks that you now face in preparing a song:

1. Text and context: the song journey
2. Vocal characterisation
3. Physical characterisation
4. Musical style and structure
5. Mapping out your song

Text and context are, I hope, self-explanatory. You will need to analyse the text of the song and the context in which it appears in the show. Sometimes you can discard the context and use your own, but you should do the research anyway.

Vocal characterisation is extremely important. It is absolutely no good singing the way you always sing and acting your socks off in the hope that it will come over! You have to make decisions about your voice quality. If you are playing a young and innocent girl, you will not want to sing with the voice quality of a mature 40-year old woman. If you are playing a sparky, sassy character, it will not be appropriate to use your ballad voice, and so on. Text and context – what is known as the 'song journey' – will also have implications for voice quality. Within the song that you are singing there will be changes of intention, intensity and tactics. You will want to depict these changes in your voice quality; this is part of your toolbox for bringing about changes in the audience, helping them to suspend their disbelief.

Physical characterisation should be approached as for a character in a play. There is sometimes a difference in working with music because of the structuring of the song and the rhythmic patterning. You will not find yourself as free to move when you want to as if it were a spoken piece: the timing is different. (This is less so with contemporary dramatic musicals such as *Les Misérables* and *Falsettoland*.) David Craig gives good guidelines on this topic.

You must take into consideration the musical style of the piece. You would not want to sing the songs from *Rent* in the same style as *Les Misérables*, or again, as in *Carousel*. A certain style of vocal production is implied in each of these genres, and you must be ready to meet their needs. Being aware of the musical structure of the piece is enormously important. It can give you valuable clues for interpretation. When there is a change of direction in the music: a new section, a repeat of previous material, a leitmoif, a dramatic key or tempo change, it always means something. This is as important to you as the verse structuring in Shakespeare, and you should not ignore it!

Mapping out your song is the culmination of this process; once you have made the decisions, you will have a map of emotional changes and the voice qualities that go with them, which will take you through the song.

POINTERS FOR WORKING THE TEXT: MEANING, PHRASING, DICTION

Meaning: the song journey

Prepare your text in detail just as you would a speech. This includes looking at the function of the song within the context of the entire musical. I spent several years working as a freelance at the East 15 Acting School and learned there about 'the 5 W's':

1. WHO? (Who are you? Know your age, your status, gender and so on.)
2. WHY? (Why are you singing the song? What do you want to achieve by the end of it? How is that a useful stepping stone in the larger journey of the play or musical?)
3. WHAT? (What exactly are you saying in the song?)
4. WHERE? (Where are you when you sing? Be as specific as you can.)
5. WHEN? (When does the song occur? What has happened before and after the song?)

Generally I find that the actor who can answer these questions will have a good basis for both a character and a song journey. If you are preparing a song from a musical, then you should know the answers to these questions within the context of the musical play, but you may well choose to use your own story to provide a different or simply more personal answer to the questions. This is particularly useful when you are auditioning, because it enables you to reveal something about yourself to the auditioning panel.

Let's look at the text of Sondheim's 'Anyone Can Whistle'. Going through 'the 5 W's' is something that you should do for yourself, taking the trouble to write down your answers. Without giving you a reading of the song, I want to point out some questions that frequently arise from the text whenever I'm preparing it with an actor.

> **Anyone can whistle, that's what they say – Easy.**
> **Anyone can whistle, any old day – Easy.**
> **It's all so simple: relax, let go, let fly.**
> **So someone tell me why can't I?**
>
> **I can dance a tango, I can read Greek – Easy.**
> **I can slay a dragon any old week – Easy.**
> **What's hard is simple.**
> **What's natural comes hard.**
> **Maybe you could show me how to let go,**
> **Lower my guard, learn to be free,**
> **Maybe if you whistle, whistle for me.**

1. Who are 'they'?
2. Who are you talking to?
3. When are you quoting and when commenting?
4. Notice at which point the words move to the first person - this is a significant change.
5. What changes for the singer in the course of the song?
6. What changes for the audience in the course of the song?
7. What's your mood at the beginning? At the end?
8. Is whistling a metaphor for life, for love, or for anything specific that you find difficult?

If I work a song like this in a workshop, I will get as many different answers as I have students in the class.

Phrasing and punctuation

Sometimes in a song there is a dichotomy between the musical phrasing and the word-phrasing or punctuation. You want to make this a dialogue if possible. If you were learning a piece of text, you would never dream of ignoring the commas and full stops, but somehow we think this is OK in singing. There are occasions when the musical phrasing seduces us away from the scanning of the text. If a song is well written, this should not happen, but not every song is perfectly constructed. In this instance, you find yourself in the middle of a pitched battle between the composer and the lyricist, and you must work your way through it to reach the audience.

In 'Anyone Can Whistle', the punctuation is quite precise, indicating when you are quoting other people and when you are speaking for yourself. Compare the musical phrasing with the word phrasing and notice when they are not quite the same. Even if you do not read music very well, you will spot some discrepancies between the way the words are said and the musical setting:

1. Look at the musical phrasing of 'Relax, let go, let fly.' It would be easy to sing straight through this. Don't; do it as you would say it, and mark the commas vocally by making a small stop at each comma. You don't need to take a breath; just stop the sound. These spaces between the notes gives the audience time to absorb what you are saying.

2. Look at unstressed syllables that are set to long notes, e.g. 'whistle', 'simple', 'natural'. If you want the audience to listen to the message of the song, rather than to your voice, you will need to use decay. (See Chapter 11, page 148.)

3. Now look at the number of ways the composer has set the word 'easy'; I believe this is a conscious choice on the composer's part. Sometimes it falls, following the inflection of the word; sometimes it rises, and in one place it leaps up through an octave. There are as many ways to inflect the word 'easy' as there are to say 'yes' and 'no' depending on your motivation. For example:

i. 'Easy': I've been doing it all my life!

ii. 'Easy': it would be if I knew how.

iii. 'Easy': I really want to impress you.

iv: 'Easy': surely everyone knows that!

Whether or not you decay, maintain a stable dynamic, or make a crescendo on these notes, should be determined by how you want to interpret the text.

Diction

You should go through the song working the diction in the way I showed you in Chapter 11. Start by counting the sound targets in each word, as we did for 'Time Heals Ev'rything' in Chapter 9. Write the number under each syllable.

Here's a reminder of the other main points from Chapter 11:

1. Beware of running words into each other that do not belong together, e.g. 'it-sall so simple'.

2. Sing the vowels that you would speak (Standard British or American), medialising any vowels that are not front vowels.

3. Write in where you need to do a glottal onset and where you need to make a stop (commas).

4. Underline your nasal consonants so that you are aware of opening

and closing the nasal port.

5. Sing the voiced consonants on pitch, paying particular attention to those on high notes.

6. Make space for the voiceless stops; remember that you will have to rob time to make them.

I have made two scores of the first sixteen bars of the song, with all these points marked except for medialising the vowels.

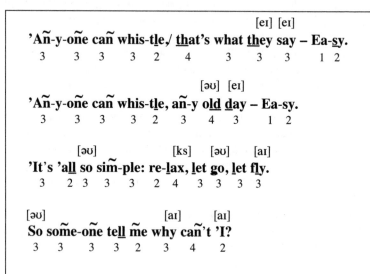

Code:

1. Phonetics of supertext for compound vowels are for Standard British.

2. Numbers below text indicate the number of sounds to be sung in each syllable.

3. A ~ indicates a nasal consonant, and therefore an open nasal port.

4. Underlining indicates a voiced consonant.

5. ' indicates a glottal onset; you could also choose to separate words from one another by a simultaneous onset.

6. '/' indicates a stop to mark the punctuation.

7. The 'x' of 'relax' is made up of two sounds: 'k' and 's'. Do not aspirate after the 'k'; hold the tongue against the soft palate in the 'k' position so that there is a silence before the 's'. (Make sure you do the same thing when you sing the music score.)

The music score above contains all the information about the vowels and consonants, and how to make your diction listener-orientated. It looks pretty scary, so I'm going to take you through it step by step.

1. Look at the music as it is normally set out on page 172.

2. Now look at this score, and see what you have to do to make yourself understood.

3. Notice how much more space the singing score takes up from left to right; every consonant and every vowel has been given its own space in the music.

4. Read it through making the sounds as you see them; do it really slowly.

5. Now sing it, still at a thinking-reading speed using the melody, but in any comfortable key. (You have to know the notes to be able to do this.)

6. Do not attempt to increase speed until you have done this several times.

7. When you have found a working speed, singing the song in the written key.

One of the things you will notice as you go through this process is that the vocal line is continually being interrupted, as well as the breath. That's the way it is. Once you put words to music, the phrasing cannot be instrumental. This is not because Sondheim has written the music inaccurately; this is the way music is usually written for singers. It is up to us to re-interpret the music so that time is allowed for all the sounds in each word. Looking at the score on page 175, you can probably appreciate why we leave this skill to the performer rather than writing it into the music each time!

Making choices – vocal characterisation

Once you have done the text work and looked at the musical structure and implications of style, you should go back to the song journey. What voice quality best conveys to the audience your psychological state at any point in the song? Go back to the questions I asked when we first looked at the text on pages 171-172. You may well want to ask more questions than the ones I have given; they are only the beginning of a process. The answers will vary from actor to actor, and from production to production. Make sure your question-answer routine is simple and direct. Here is a more detailed list of the factors you could be considering:

1. Questions. Who am I? What do I want? How am I going to get it? What is in my way? Where am I? Why am I here? When is it? What am I doing? What is my action?

2. Internal factors. What are my needs and desires? What is my social background? Ethnic values? Physiology? Psychological peculiarities or ways of thinking of the character?

3. External factors. What are my relationships with, or attitudes towards, other characters? (In some interpretations of a song, this may only involve the person to whom the song is directed.) What is my social environment? Physical environment? Are there any specific immediate circumstances to take into consideration?

I'm now going to give you two very broad outlines for a journey through the song, leaving you to fill in your own specifics. You'll find that different voice qualities are implied in each version of the song. Remember that the choice of voice qualities is a subjective one; you may well go for something quite opposite to the ones I've given, based on your own story and changes of intention. That is absolutely fine: the point is to make decisions. Remember that in this song you are quoting what others say, commenting on what they say, and expressing your own feelings. All of these might be indicated by a change of voice quality. Some voice qualities work better in certain parts of the range than others. There are differences between male and female voices in this respect, e.g. falsetto does not read well low in the male voice, and men can take speech quality higher more easily than women. It's possible my choices will not work well in your voice, but you will get the idea from looking at these song maps, and will be able to come up with your own solutions.

Journey 1
At the beginning you are resentful and cynical. (Ask yourself, who are they trying to kid?) You move into bravado for the second section. (Tell them you can do this and that.) Then you become more thoughtful and vulnerable, with a big change on the word 'maybe'. But that is too much for you, and you finish the song in cynical mode.

Overleaf is a short score of the music (words and text only) indicating the changes of voice quality that would go with this scenario.

Journey 2
At the beginning of the song you are uncertain and wistful. (You think of what you wish you could do too.) You begin to encourage and cheer yourself. (You think of the things you can do.) You become more positive, hopeful and open. (Life isn't what I expected, but you can see there are people around to help.)

The voice qualities indicated would be somewhat different.

Looking over the two journeys and word scores, you may be wondering why I haven't told you where to breathe. Quite often this will be the first thing a singer marks in on the vocal score. I think it should be the last if it is needed at all! If you are making the consonants correctly and energetically, you will find that you can take a breath *anywhere you like*. If then, for the purposes of audience communication, you want to signal that you have taken a breath, you can do so by increasing the length of your silence as you breathe, of by making your breath audible. For example, in the phrase 'so someone tell me why can't I?', which is actually

one of the longest phrases in the song, you could breathe on the 't' of 'can't'. These is an aspirate after the 't' when it is made properly, and no-one will notice that you took a breath. You can even use the same ploy at the beginning of words if you are in need of breath; put your hand over the abdomen at the naval as you sing the 's' of 'someone' and 't' of 'tell me'. Do it energetically and you will be taking in involuntary breath. At this point in your training, that's really all that needs to be said about breathing as part of song preparation.

Musical style and structure

Written in 1964, this is the title song from the show *Anyone Can Whistle*. I won't attempt to give you the synopsis; it's too complicated, and you can easily look it up for yourself. The setting is contemporary and there is nothing that indicates a particular vocal style. Structurally, there are two verses and a coda (finishing off section), but the song is constructed to give a through-composed feel rather than of two verses.

Mapping out your song

Mapping out the song is a way of making sure you know what you are doing. Once you have understood the structure of the music and its dramatic implications, you can mark in on the score each change of intention that requires a change in voice quality. It doesn't just have to be broad strokes; if it's appropriate, you can change voice quality in the middle of a word and several times in a musical phrase.

You should now make your own map of the song, using either the musical or word score (whichever is easiest the read), writing in all the changes of thought and voice quality, and any subtext that is personal to you.

Song assignment 1: WITH EVERY BREATH I TAKE

Here is a song from Cy Coleman's *City of Angels* (lyrics by David Zippel). In the show it is sung by a woman, but the text isn't gender-specific so a man could sing it too. In fact, it's a song that could be sung by anybody about a relationship that has been. Here's the text:

A section

There's not a morning that I open up my eyes
and find I didn't dream of you.
Without a warning, though it's never a surprise,
soon as I awake,
thoughts of you arise
with ev'ry breath I take.

Bridge section

At any time or place I close my eyes and see your face
and I'm embracing you.
If only I believed that dreams come true.
Darling,

A section

You were the one who said forever from the start and I've been
drifting since you've gone,
out on a lonely sea that only you can chart.
I've been going on
knowing that my heart will break
with every breath I take.

I've chosen this song to work on because it is written in a very traditional ABA form. It would be easy to perform this song as a torch song for an unresolved lost love, but it can be read another way too.

There is, for instance, no need to let the audience know until you sing the word 'if' that all is not well. You could start the song in a state of happy luxuriance, enjoying the feelings that this person evokes in you, until you bring yourself up short in the final section. Cy Coleman has cleverly made the music overlap into this section to fool the audience for a little longer. So, if this is the outline of your scenario, what voice qualities are implied?

Remember that different voice qualities will mean different things in a different setting, and even a 'happy' voice quality can change if it is delivered with sarcasm, so what I'm offering here is will again be subjective. Voice qualities indicating a state of happiness might be:

1. falsetto quality (soft, sexy and intimate);
2. cry quality mixed with speech (warm and deep);
3. cry quality on its own (very soft and silky tone).

The tempo is slow, so I don't feel twang is indicated; the feel would be too upbeat. Pay special attention to the last line of the first section 'with ev'ry breath I take', because you are going to repeat it at the end of the song with a totally different emphasis. You might want to make this line extra soft in dynamic, or change quality for it. Within the overall quality you choose for the section, a change of quality might be indicated when you have a sub-clause qualifying what you have just said: '(though it's never a surprise)'.

The bridge section needs to build in intensity: the feelings become more pressing, real and immediate. This is reflected in the rising melodic line of the music so you need to go with it:

1. If you started in falsetto, you might like to move to cry with speech (intensity and warmth).
2. If you started in cry (or mixed it with speech), you might want to move into twang. Remember that you can add twang to any voice quality (except falsetto) to increase its intensity.
3. Within this overall change there are words and phrases where you might want a different quality, e.g. at the words 'and I'm embracing you'.
4. What ever you decide, there must be a change at the word 'if'. Remember that to get suddenly soft and breathy can be just as shocking as changing to a louder voice quality. (Think of people who go quiet when they are angry!)

The last section could be construed as accusatory, sarcastic, bitter:
1. Speech quality can be angry, especially when mixed with twang.
2. Twang on its own could be sarcastic.
3. The short phrases that build to the end ('I've been going on, knowing that my heart will break') need to build to a climax, and belt quality is indicated here. (Men who are not basses will want this song transposed up a little in

order to get the belt. The pitch is too low otherwise to make this quality.)

4. After the belt, you must decide how you want to deliver the last line. What effect do you want to have on the audience or person to whom the song is addressed? You could choose:

i. speech quality for resignation;

ii. falsetto quality for regret or a sigh;

iii. speech and twang for anger;

iv. cry quality for a sense of wallowing in your feelings.

Song assignment 2: IF THE HEART OF A MAN (MEN); WHEN MY HERO IN COURT APPEARS (WOMEN)

Both these songs are from John Gay's *The Beggar's Opera*. The first is sung by Macheath, quite early on in the opera, before he is tricked by Polly's parents. The second is sung by Polly Peachum as she tries to

dissuade her father from going ahead with arraigning her lover. For this exercise, I want you to work backwards, i.e. to make the voice qualities I have suggested *before* you have made any decisions about text and character. You should work this exercise with a friend of with a tape recorder. If you do this with a friend, they should not watch you while you are singing, but listen to you as in a radio performance. What psychological states were conveyed through the voice qualities you used? Did they have the effect you expected? If not, explore or discuss what might be changed in order to create the response you want in the listener.

The act of singing involves many things: your craft as a singer, your ability to make clear your intentions and psychological states to the audience, the raw material of the song, and the composer's intention. All of these have to be fused to make a performance. Some aspects of

the work with voice qualities may seem somewhat dry in approach to the magical act of performing! I know of actors who feel that mapping out the song in this way will stifle their creativity and stop them from 'being in the moment'. If you have made your decisions and carry them out with 500% commitment, you will stay in the moment, and so will the audience. Decisions about voice quality enable you to repeat this process eight times a week and to recreate the moment as if it were new every time.

Singing is a craft and an art, *not* just a gift. All good artists need to learn their craft before moving onto the creative act of performance. The aim of this book has been to show you how to learn and practise your craft. Magic in performance can come at any time, but as you perfect your craft, it's likely to happen more often. My philosophy is that knowledge dispels fear. You cannot be a truly confident performer if you are unsure of what you are doing. My hope is that, having read this book, you will know and do more.

Enjoy!

GLOSSARY

Alveolar ridge The ridge of gum behind the upper front teeth.

Arytenoid cartilages Small pyramid shaped structures that sit on the shoulders of the cricoid cartilage. The back of the vocal folds attach to them.

Cervical spine The first seven vertebrae of the spinal column.

Changes of registration The points where the vocal folds change length and thickness.

Connective tissue This exists around the muscles in the body enabling them to move smoothly.

Cry/Sob quality Defined by Jo Estill as defined as low larynx. *Cry* is a variation of *Sob* quality, which is currently less used in Musical Theatre singing.

The Estill model A model for voice-training devised by the American researcher and teacher Jo Estill. The core course titles are *Compulsory Figures for Voice* (Level One) and *Six Voice Qualities* (Level Two). In the UK this body of work goes under the generic title *Voice Craft*. There is an *EVTS* website for information about training courses and licensed teachers of the model: http://www.evts.com

False vocal folds These consist of tissue and fatty matter, and their function is to make a tight seal in the larynx to protect the airways.

Falsetto quality For this quality, Jo Estill specifies a posteriorly raised vocal fold plane, which I have not included here. This is not intended as a departure from the Estill model; it is in recognition of current performance practice in theatre singing – that many actors use a variation of falsetto quality that is not necessarily raised plane.

Fricatives These sounds are characterised by a continuous airstream passing through an obstructed vocal tract.

Glottal This means 'of the glottis'.

Glottis This is a notional term, referring to the space between the vocal folds. Hence we close the glottis when we make sound, open it when we are breathing in.

Harmonic A component frequency of wave motion.

Hertz The unit of frequency (number of cycles per second).

Isolation checklist A sequence of physical movements devised to help you isolate muscles used in tasks.

Larynx The thyroid and cricoid cartilages, the epiglottis and the hyoid bone. (The larynx is sometimes referred to as the 'voice box'.)

Leitmotif A short musical or rhythmic phrase that is used to represent a character or specific emotion.

Mandible The jaw bone.

Masseter The muscle that raises the mandible.

Maxilla The gum bone.

Nasal port The doorway between the nasal and oral cavities (also called the velar-pharyngeal port).

Occipital groove The depression at the base of the skull.

Onset The start of sound; in singing it refers to specifically how we bring the vocal folds together.

Palato-glossus The muscle linking the back of the tongue and soft palate used to lift the back of the tongue upwards for sounds such as 'k'.

Palato pharyngeus A paired muscle of the soft palate that helps to raise the larynx in swallowing.

Passaggio This is Italian for 'passage' and describes a point of transition in the vocal range.

Pharynx The tube of the vocal tract.

Pilates system A complete approach to developing body awareness and an easy physicality in day-to-day life, recommended by health experts as a safe form of exercise.

Plosive A class of sound characterised by a complete occlusion of the vocal tract; there is a build up of pressure, followed by release.

Retraction A term coined by Jo Estill to describe the movement of the false vocal folds in the silent laugh posture. At this point in time, we do not know what causes the false vocal folds to move away from the mid-line; we simply know that it happens.

Simple vowels Single vowel sounds (also called monophthongs); they can be either long or short.

Siren An exercise taken by Jo Estill from Lilli Lehman's book *How to Sing*, and developed to work on vocal awareness and range. The sound is made in imitation a police or ambulance siren, hence the name.

Spectrogram A visual record of sound energy and quality.

Subglottic pressure The pressure of air beneath the vocal folds.

Supra-hyoid The muscles and structure above the hyoid bone.

TMJ The temporo mandibular joint: the hinge of the jaw.

Vibratory cycle The disturbance of air which makes up the sound source.

Zygoma The cheekbone.

LIST OF GENERAL EXERCISES, AWARENESS EXERCISES AND SONG ASSIGNMENTS

Chapter 1
Awareness exercise 1: the vibrating mechanism
Awareness exercise 2: closing the vocal folds
Awareness exercise 3: locating the soft palate
Awareness exercise 4: the siren

Chapter 2
Awareness exercise 1: constricting the larynx
Exercise 1: retraction
Awareness exercise 2: the glottal onset
Awareness exercise 3: the aspirate onset
Awareness exercise 4: the simultaneous onset

Chapter 3
Awareness exercise 1: general awareness
Awareness exercise 2: feeling the larynx
Awareness exercise 3: raising and lowering your larynx
Awareness exercise 4: moving the larynx forwards and backwards
Awareness exercise 5: tilting the thyroid
Awareness exercise 6: tilting the cricoid

Chapter 4
Awareness exercise 1: reviewing onset of tone
Awareness exercise 2: monitoring airflow
Awareness exercise 3: consonants
Exercise 1: the elastic recoil
Exercise 2: working the recoil with rhythm
Awareness exercise 4: the waistband
Awareness exercise 5: the abdominal wall (top and bottom)
Awareness exercise 6: the diamond
Exercise 3: working to sustain

Chapter 5
Exercise 1: laughing at the larynx
Exercise 2: random sirening
Exercise 3: targeting your breaks
Exercise 4: octave sirens
Exercise 5: from siren to vowel
Exercise 6: feeling the pitch
Song assignment: your song

Exercise 6: lengthening the vocal tract with the lips
Song assignment 3: your song

Chapter 9
Exercise 1: preparation for twang
Exercise 2: accessing twang
Exercise 3: twanging
Exercise 4: twanging with all vowels
Exercise 5: oral twang
Song assignment: *Amazing Grace*

Chapter 10
Song assignment: your song

Chapter 11
Exercise 1: vocal line
Exercise 2: consonants
Exercise 3: coming off voiced consonants
Exercise 4: analyse your own song
Exercise 5: listening

Chapter 12
Exercise 1: steps to speech quality
Exercise 2: steps to falsetto quality
Exercise 3: steps to cry quality
Exercise 4: comparing cry and twang
Exercise 5: comparing effort levels for speech, twang and cry
Exercise 6: comparing speech and falsetto
Exercise 7: preparation for belting
Exercise 8: effort for belting
Song assignment 1: belting
Song assignment 2: whose song is it anyway?

Chapter 13
Song assignment 1: *With Every Breath I Take*
Song assignment 2: *If the Heart of a Man* (men) / *When My Hero in Court
Appears* (women)

INDEX

INDEX OF SONG TITLES